W9-BRP-305

Gender-Specific Aspects of Human Biology for the Practicing Physician

by

Marianne J. Legato, M.D., F.A.C.P.
Associate Professor of Clinical Medicine
at the
Columbia University College
of Physicians and Surgeons

Futura Publishing Company, Inc.
Armonk, NY

Library of Congress Cataloging-in-Publication Data

Legato, Marianne J., 1935–
    Gender-specific aspects of human biology for the practicing
physician / by Marianne J. Legato
        p. cm.
    Includes bibliographical references and index
    ISBN 0-87993-648-7
    1. Sex differences.   2. Sex factors in disease.   3. Women—
Health and hygiene.   4. Women—Diseases.   I. Title
    [DNLM: 1. Sex Characteristics.   QT 104 L498g 1996]
QP81.5.L44   1996
612.6—dc20
DNLM/DLC
for Library of Congress   96-32122
                                                CIP

Copyright © 1997
Futura Publishing Company, Inc.

Published by
Futura Publishing Company, Inc.
135 Bedford Raod
Armonk, New York 10504-0418

LC #: 96-32122
ISBN #: 0-87993-648-7

Every effort has been made to ensure that the information in this
book is as up to date and as accurate as possible at the time of
publication. However, due to the constant developments in
medicine, neither the author, nor the editor, nor the publisher can
accept any legal or any other responsibility for any errors or
omissions that may occur.

Printed in the United States of America.

This book is printed on acid-free paper.

Dedication

For

T George Harris

and

Craig B. Wynett

Acknowledgements

The author gratefully acknowledges the intelligent and constructive advice of Mr. Steven Korn which was so important in the preparation of this book. Ms. Benita Marks' hours of computer searching were invaluable in assembling the information reported here. The meticulous editing of Ms. Marcy H. Kroll helped refine the final product. Finally, the interest of the Procter & Gamble corporation in the health of women throughout the world proved an essential resource and support for the research necessary to produce this volume.

Foreword

In recent years, research relating to women's health has been increasingly recognized as a priority area for medical and scientific investigation and, in the fashion of so many important causes, has become politicized. These are important happenings: it is clear that without an understanding of the scientific basis for the differences between the sexes in biology and in disease and the means to disseminate this understanding among the medical and the general populace, scientific dicovery cannot be translated into effective measures for advancing health care. The politicization is, as always, a two-edged sword; needed as a means to popularize, yet leading to smudging, if not flat-out redrawing of the line between accuracy and hyperbole.

Any rapidly growing field can only benefit from the leadership of individuals who are equally schooled in the science and the practice of medicine, as well as possessed of the skills to evaluate and communicate information in ways that are understandable to the general medical and lay communities. In the area of women's health, this role is admirably filled by Dr. Marianne J. Legato. Her career has been one of excellence in basic scientific research, witnessed by over twenty years of publications in the leading specialty journals, and complemented by clinical achievements for which she has received acclaim as a teacher as well as a practitioner of medicine.

Dr. Legato, long an authority on developmental biology, recognized some years ago that gender is an important determinant of physiology in ways far more diverse than the generally recognized reproductive biology. She then began the difficult learning process required of one who is to master a new and far-ranging field. The expertise she attained has received recognition through the acclaim of her earlier books, her service on government panels, her appearances in the media, and her role in advancing the cause of women's health.

Perhaps uniquely among those who champion the issue of women's health, Dr Legato has advanced the hypothesis that it is not women's research alone, but rather, gender-specific research, that will best provide advances in basic science and its application to health care and to education. Hence, her approach in general, and in this volume, in particular, is to consider both the female and the male as counterpoints to one another, reacting physiologically and pathophysiologically in comparable fashion in some settings and very disparately in others. Dr. Legato's understanding of gonadal steroid effects on fundamental cellular processes in the diverse systems of the body provides her with the background to discuss the similar and the dissimilar reactions of the male and the female to aging and to disease. It is not so much a matter of extrapolating information gained on males to the care of females (long the practice of medicine worldwide) or vice versa, but rather the gathering of information for each and then considering that which is concordant and that which is discordant which will make a difference.

In her discussion of the gender-related determinants of physiology and pathophysiology, Dr. Legato covers a wide range of subject matter: literally the entire gamut from brains, bones and breasts to hearts and halitosis is commented on, as are aspects of pharmacology and of metabolism. Hence, the physician seeking to understand not only Dr. Legato's views on these areas but seeking access to a variety of reference sources is appropriately guided and directed. The book reads well, makes even the drier areas of investigation understandable and palatable, and should be a welcomed addition to the library of the compleat physician.

Michael R. Rosen. M.D.
New York, New York

Contents

Chapter 1

Bone

Osteoporosis: Epidemiology and Economics

The cost of osteoporosis is sobering: we pay $10 billion for it annually and unless the present trends change, medical expenses associated with osteoporosis will exceed $30 billion by 2020.[1] In 20 years there will be approximately half a million hip fractures a year. This is a serious health problem: hip fracture increases mortality 12-20% within the first year compared to controls and 15-20% of patients must remain in long term care institutions for at least a year. By the age of 70, 40% of women now alive will have had an osteoporosis-related fracture. By age 80, 15% of women will have had a hip fracture.[2]

Calcium Metabolism and Bone Maintenance

Bone is dynamic and is constantly being remodeled. It is resorbed and laid down under a series of controlling

1

mechanisms that depend on the interaction of osteoclasts, which resorb bone and osteoblasts, which form new bone. As osteoclasts resorb bone, they signal osteoblasts to fill the newly formed cavity with a collagen rich material, the bone matrix. The mineral phase of bone, hydroxyapatite, is then laid down and the matrix is mineralized to form new bone. Hydroxyapatite crystals contain sodium, magnesium, carbonate and citrate ions, but calcium and phosphorus are the primary components. When balanced, the process of bone remodeling results in no bone loss and no new formation. About 500 mg of calcium are turned over daily.

A subtle disturbance in this balance begins around the age of 30, when bone loss begins to exceed bone formation almost imperceptibly. This age-related bone loss is more intense in women than in men[3] and indeed, vertebral bone density, highest in young women during their second decade of life, begins to decrease significantly each decade thereafter.[4] It is interesting to note that bone mass continues to increase linearly in men until about age 26, but in young women, bone mass plateaus before age 20.[5] It is distressing that while young women may know about the importance of building maximal bone mass while they can still do so, in one study of 127 university women, only 7% were taking in the recommended amounts of dietary calcium.[6] A much more accelerated bone loss (as much as 5% a year) begins in women within 5-10 years after menopause, and occurs principally in trabecular spongy bone of which the vertebral bones are almost entirely composed. Hip bone, intermediate in composition compared with the much denser cortical bone of arms and legs (which is much less sensitive to estrogen deficiency), is also affected but not as dramatically as the backbone.

The accelerated bone loss that occurs in menopause is due to the overactivity of osteoclasts and is called type I osteoporosis. The slower, age-dependent bone loss, called type II osteoporosis, is probably the result of impaired bone formation due to underactivity of osteoblasts.[7] The two types of osteoporosis differ in many of their clinical features: type I affects women six times more frequently than men, while type II incidence predominates in women by only 2:1 versus men.

Type I Osteoporosis

The most accelerated phase of bone loss occurs immediately after menopause and begins to decline 8-10 years later. This phenomenon is not exclusively related to estrogen deficiency: only 20% of women develop osteoporotic fractures within 20 years after their menses stop.[8] These women are not necessarily more estrogen deficient than their counterparts. Other identifiable risk factors include family history, smoking, caffeine consumption, lack of physical exercise, alcohol use and the level of peak bone mass which is generated in young adult life. Alcohol inhibits osteoblastic activity and smoking decreases estrogen levels.

Parathyroid Hormone (PTH) and Osteoporosis

Another potential agent in the genesis of osteoporosis is parathyroid hormone (PTH). The role of this hormone in maintaining bone density is complex and varies with age, serum concentration and the location of the bone on which it acts. Parathyroid hormone tends to reinforce or protect cancellous bone, while it causes osteoporosis of the cortical bone of the arms and legs. In situations of PTH excess, therefore, osteoporosis develops but is not that typically seen in postmenopausal life; it is more prominent in the cortical bone of arms and legs and not in the cancellous bone of the vertebral column. In fact, PTH has a sparing effect on the cancellous bone of the vertebral column and spinal bone density is higher than that of controls in women with primary hyperparathyroidism. Some investigators are looking at the use of PTH in preventing the disabling osteoporosis of postmenopausal life.[9]

Calcium levels in the body remain constant because of the interplay of a number of factors. Calcium enters the plasma as a function of absorption by the intestine (regulated in part by the active metabolite of vitamin D, 1,25 dihydroxyvitamin D, produced in the kidney under the control of PTH). It leaves the plasma and the body by resecretion into the intestinal lumen, by renal secretion and by loss in sweat.[10] Parathyroid hormone also regulates calcium concentrations in the body through its crucial role in bone metabolism: it activates osteoblasts and, secondarily, osteoclasts. When it is increased over optimal levels, it induces excessive bone remodeling with consequent net loss of bone. Hence, its causative role in osteoporosis may be significant. This catabolic effect of PTH on bone may obscure the fact that in normal concentrations and in the premenopausal patient, it has a major anabolic action.

Kidney stones are a common complication of hyperparathyroidism; the kidney is presented with more calcium than it can adequately handle. In extreme cases, proximal muscle weakness is prominent and the patient may complain of difficulty lifting her arms to brush her hair.

The levels of PTH are decreased in type I osteoporosis, which affects women virtually exclusively and develops within 15 years after menopause. Parathyroid hormone is more easily suppressed in these patients in response to high calcium levels in the plasma and the parathyroids show a blunted response to hypocalcemia.[11] These patients also have an abnormality of vitamin D metabolism.

Type II Osteoporosis

Senile osteoporosis, which is the consequence of age-related bone loss, manifests itself later in life, and is seen clinically in patients over the age of 70. Females are more affected than males. Probably because of an impaired ability of the kidney to generate 1,25 dihydroxy vitamin D, there is decreased calcium absorbtion in these patients.

This, in turn, produces increased levels of PTH. This phenomenon is more severe in women with age-related osteoporosis.[12]

Circadian rhythms in PTH differ in men and women, and this difference has been implicated in explaining the greater bone loss women suffer compared with men.[13]

Women have a less pronounced rise in circulating PTH in response to fasting than do men, and their kidneys conserve less calcium in response to even mild food restriction (overnight fasting, for example). This minor difference may have a significant effect over the course of a lifetime.

Estrogen counteracts the action of parathyroid hormone and, in postmenopausal women not on estrogen replacement therapy (ERT), the skeleton may be more impacted by circulating levels of PTH.[14] In such patients, the bone of the cancellous spine is actually protected.

The importance of primary hyperparathyroidism is increasing and it has become a common disease in women over the past 25 years, largely due to better methods of detecting hypercalcemia. In most cases the disease is asymptomatic, and is detected on routine laboratory screening which reveals an elevated serum calcium in a patient who feels well.[15] It occurs three times more in women than in men and is most often seen within the first ten years after menopause.[16]

The cause of primary hyperparathyroidism is unknown, and usually involves the hyperfunctioning of only one of the four parathyroid glands. In some cases, all four glands are involved. Among the causes of this is a history of radiation of the neck, face and upper chest for acne, as was commonly practiced in the 1930s and 1940s. The glands may also be hyperactive as part of a syndrome of concomitant hyperfunction of the pituitary and pancreas (multiple endocrine neoplasia), but simple primary hyperthyroidism is far more common. Interestingly, postmenopausal women with primary hyperparathyroidism show a preservation of cancellous bone.[16]

Osteoporosis in Men

Spinal osteoporosis in men is related to several factors, some of which can be modified to prevent the disease. Riggs compared the clinical features of bone loss in men and women.[17] The rate of bone loss in the hip is a third more rapid in women than in men, and in the spine, men loose only a quarter of the bone density that women loose. They estimated that senile (type II) osteoporosis affects more than half the population of aging women and a fourth of aging men. In another series of 105 male patients, the most important risk factors for type II osteoporosis were smoking (relative risk [RR] 2.3), alcoholic intake (RR 2.4) and the presence of an associated medical disease known to affect calcium or bone metabolism (RR 5.5). Obesity protected men from osteoporosis (RR 0.3).[18] The risk associated with smoking and drinking accelerated with age. Risk factors were cumulative but independent of one another.

Treatment Options for Osteoporosis

Prevention

Prevention of osteoporosis starts with menarche. Young women should be encouraged to adopt a lifestyle that includes good nutrition, exercise and attention to estrogen levels.

Treatment for Type I Osteoporosis

Bilezikian advises three areas of focus for the treating physician who is fashioning a therapeutic plan for osteoporosis.[19] The first is to foster peak bone mass in young women. The second is to minimize the amount of bone lost after the patient finishes the second decade of life. Finally, the physician must decide how to restore bone mass in the osteoporotic patient without compromising the structural integrity of bone.

Calcium: How Much is Enough and When Do We Need It?

Achieving optimal peak bone mass depends on adequate nutritional factors and specifically, on the intake of enough calcium. The premenopausal woman's requirement for calcium varies with age. From 0-10 years of age, the recommendation is for 800 mg a day; in adolescence, the requirement rises to 1,200 mg. Premenopausal women need 1,000 mg a day but postmenopausal women, 1,400 mg, due to a combination of less intestinal absorption and poorer calcium reabsorption by the kidneys which is characteristic of aging.[20] If vitamin E is also administered, improved intestinal absorption results and decreases the requirement to 1,200 mg a day. These values are higher than the Recommended Daily Allowance (RDA). Since the average postmenopausal woman ingests between 450 mg and 650 mg of calcium a day, the general need is to double the amount taken in.

In the adult, ingested calcium is better absorbed if taken in small amounts.[21] Absorption occurs in the duodenum and proximal jejunum and in most women, is complete within 4 hours of ingestion. Adults absorb only 30-50% of the ingested dose.[22] The amount of calcium, and not the source, is the determinant of calcium balance; it does not matter whether or not the patient uses milk or supplements to achieve desirable intake levels.[23] In choosing calcium supplements, it is important to know that only elemental calcium is absorbed. Among the salts available to patients—calcium carbonate, lactate, gluconate and citrate—some investigators feel that calcium citrate is more available.[24] Since solubility is directly related to absorption, a reasonably effective preparation will dissolve in vinegar within 30 minutes.[25] Multiple doses are less likely to saturate the intestinal absorption mechanisms, and doses taken in the evening are more likely to amplify the amount needed. Calcium release is diurnal; it is stored in the bone during the day and released during sleep.[26] Impaired gastric acidity, which is frequent in postmenopausal women, interferes with calcium absorption, so calcium carbonate salts are best taken with a meal. Women at risk for renal stones should only take calcium citrate, which inhibits calcium oxalate crystallization.[27]

Whether or not calcium alone has an impact on preventing osteoporosis depends on several factors: the total amount of calcium taken in across the pre-, peri- and postmenopausal years (rather than any calcium intake at one isolated period) and adequate estrogen levels. Adequate dietary calcium throughout life is associated with fewer osteoporosis-related fractures; women who ingest over 765 mg a day have a 60% lower risk of hip fracture.[28] Dietary calcium intake in women is not as well correlated with current bone density, as is that of men. In men, dietary calcium intake was a reliable predictor of vulnerability to osteoporosis,[29] and hence of fractures: dietary calcium explained 24-42% of the variance at lumbar spine and femoral neck, respectively. The lack of correlation between vulnerability to injury and dietary calcium intake in women was probably a reflection of the much greater variability of intake over the course of a lifetime in women.[30]

Intake of fat-soluble vitamin D, which is activated in sun-exposed skin, can be deficient in low fat diets, in patients with malabsorption of fats, and in elderly people not exposed to sunlight. An adequate amount of vitamin D is 400 IU per day (the amount in a multivitamin).[31] Excessive vitamin D increases renal calcium excretion and promotes cortical bone loss.[32]

Exercise

In moderation, exercise enhances bone density. Optimal exercise programs must involve antigravity exertion but avoid stress on mechanical sites like knees and elbows; running, therefore, is not always beneficial. In women who are already osteoporotic, special care must be used so that fractures and other injuries to bone are avoided. Finally, an excess of exercise which is sufficient to produce amenorrhea is harmful and promotes bone resorption due to estrogen deficiency.[33]

To be useful, exercise programs must be continued for relatively long periods of time.[34,35] It is interesting that a 12-month program of walking in one study did not prevent bone loss in postmenopausal women,[36] and drop-out rates of even very supportive exercise programs are high.[37] Weight training seems to be effective in increasing bone density, but the gains are lost once exercise is stopped.[38]

Estrogen

Estrogen therapy has a bone-conserving effect no matter when in life it is started.[39] Low estrogen levels produce an increase in local cytokines, particularly interleukin 6; this stimulates osteoclasts to multiply and increases the intensity of their activity.[40] Optimal doses for conserving bone are 1-2 mg of estradiol[41] or 0.625 mg of conjugated bovine estrogen daily.[42] Micronized 17 beta-estradiol maintained bone mass and increased it in doses of 1-2 mg, as did doses of 15-25 mg of ethinyl estradiol.[43] Because absorption differs, especially if the patch is used, women's serum concentration of estrogen should be monitored and levels kept above 40-60 pg/mL for maximum bone protection. Estrogen replacement protects bone in amenorrheic athletes.[44]

Estrogen therapy must, of course, be individualized: use for 15 or more years is associated with an increased risk of breast cancer,[45] and women with a history of breast cancer in their families or themselves should be carefully monitored during estrogen replacement therapy (ERT). A history of breast cancer is not an absolute contraindication, however; women can be carefully monitored at 6-month intervals for breast malignancy and may be more at risk from osteoporosis and/or coronary artery disease, risks that are reduced by ERT. Other relative contraindications to ERT include migraine headaches, fibroid tumors, endometriosis and, in some cases, hypertension. An absolute contraindication to ERT is a hypercoagulable state with the appearance of thrombophlebitis; there is an increased risk for pulmonary embolism in such patients.

Progestins stimulate bone formation (estrogen works principally by decreasing bone resorption) and may be used synergistically with estrogen replacement.[46,47] Calcium in adequate amounts promotes estrogen effect, and dosages of 1,500 mg a day may lower the required dose for maintaining bone mass.[48]

Addition of low-dose androgen to an estrogen replacement program may be a useful new therapeutic direction. Androgen helps stimulate bone formation in postmenopausal women; estrogen alone, while it diminishes bone resorption, also decreases new bone formation.[49] By the ninth week of receiving methyltestosterone, a small series of women showed an increase of 24% of osteocalcin levels, a marker of new bone formation. This was in contrast to women on estrogen only, who showed a 40% decrease in the marker.[50] Similar trends were noted for alkaline phosphatase, another marker of new bone formation. (For further information on estrogen replacement therapy, see Chapters 3 and 5.)

Calcitonin

This hormone inhibits osteoclasts and, therefore, bone resorption. It has a similar role to estrogen and in studies looking at its use for short periods, seemed to prevent early postmenopausal bone loss (within two to three years of menopause).[51,52] Calcitonin is unlikely to be useful until cheaper analogues become available.[53]

Fluoride

Initial results with sodium fluoride in strengthening bone were not encouraging. Gastrointestinal complaints were frequent and the bone that was produced seemed to have inferior structural properties; although mass was increased, fractures were no less frequent.[54] More recent work with a slow release sodium fluoride preparation seems to hold promise; using this medication, bone was normally mineralized and seemed structurally sound.[55]

Etiodronate

Two well-designed studies showed that etiodronate increases vertebral bone density and it did not seem to so at the expense of cortical bone.[56,57] Recently, however, the FDA has disapproved the use of the drug for use in osteoporosis, unconvinced that it reduced the number of fractures in this condition.

Treatment for Senile Osteoporosis (Type II)

In type II osteoporosis, the best available data seem to indicate that calcium supplementation stabilizes bone loss and may even improve mineralization. Modest amounts of vitamin D should be prescribed (400 IU is sufficient). There are no studies that prove estrogen replacement that is initiated over the age of 75 has any impact on the incidence of hip fracture. Such a study, in fact, is not feasible. Ettinger points out that it would require a large cohort of women of at least age 75 to be studied prospectively for 25 years, to establish whether or not estrogen is beneficial.[58] For similar reasons, there is no sound experimental basis for using calcitonin in the treatment of type II osteoporosis.

References

1. Miller CW. Survival and ambulation following hip fractures. J Bone Joint Surg Am. 1978;60:930-934.

2. Bilezikian JP and Silverberg SH. Osteoporosis: a practical approach to the perimenopausal woman. J Women's Health. 1991;1:21-27.
3. Eriksen EF, Mosekilde L, Melson F. Trabecular bone resorption depth decreases with age: differences between normal males and females. Bone. 1985;6:141-146.
4. Buchanan JR, Myers C., Lloyd T, Greer RB III. Early vertebral trabecular bone loss in normal premenopausal women. J Bone Miner Res 1988;3:583-587.
5. Gordon CL, Halton JM, Atkinson SA, Webber CE. The contributions of growth and puberty to peak bone mass. Growth Dev Aging. 1991;55:257-262.
6. Kasper MJ, Peterson MGE, Allegrante JP, et al. Knowledge, beliefs and behaviors among college women concerning the prevention of osteoporosis. Arch Fam Med. 1994;3:696-702.
7. Erikson EF, Mosekilde L, Melsen F. Trabecular bone resorption depth decreases with age: differences between normal males and females. Bone. 1985;6:141-146.
8. Riggs B, Melton L. Medical progress: involutional osteoporosis. N Engl J Med. 1986;314:1676-1686.
9. Lindsay RL, Cosman F. Primary osteoporosis. In: Coe FL, Favus MJ eds. Disorders of Bone and Mineral Metabolism. New York: Raven Press. 1992.
10. Holick MF, Krane SM, Potts JT. Calcium, phosphorus and bone metabolism: calcium-regulating hormones. In: Harrison's Principles of Internal Medicine. 12th ed. New York: McGraw-Hill, Inc; 1991:1894-1895.
11. Silverberg S, Shane E, de la Cruz L, Segre G, Clemens T, Bilezikian J. Abnormalities in parathyroid hormone secretion and 1,25 dihydroxvitamin D, formation in women with osteoporosis. N Engl J Med. 1989;320:277-281.
12. Tsai K, Heath H, Kuman R, Riggs B. Impaired vitamin D metabolism with aging in women. J Clin Invest. 1984;73:1668-1672.
13. Calvo MS, Eastell R, Offord KP, Bergstralh EJ, Burritt MF. Circadian variation in ionized calcium and intact

parathyroid hormone: evidence for sex differences in calcium homeostasis. J Clin Endocrinol Metab. 1991;72:77-82.

14. Silverberg SJ, Bilezikian JP. Parathyroid function and responsiveness in osteoporosis. In: Bilezikian JP, Levine MA, Marchus R, eds. The Parathyroids. New York: Raven Press, Ltd; 1994:805-812.

15. Bilezikian JP. Primary hyperparathyroidism: another important metabolic bone disease of women. J Wom Health. 1994;3:21-32.

16. Bilezikian JP, Silverberg SJ, Shane E, Parisien M, Dempster DW. Characterization and evaluation of asymptomatic primary hyperparathyroidism. J Bone Min Res. 1991;6:585-589.

17. Riggs BL, Wahner H, Seeman E, Offord K, Dunn W, Mazess R, Johnson K, Melton L. Changes in bone mineral density of the proximal femur and spine with aging. J Clin Invest. 1982;70:716-723.

18. Seeman E, Melton LD, O'Fallon WM, Riggs BL. Risk factors for spinal osteoporosis in men. Am J Med. 1983;75:977-983.

19. Bilezikian JP. Osteoporosis: on the verge of rational effective therapy? Mt Sinai J Med. 1993;60:87-94.

20. Heaney RP, Gallagher JC, Johnston CC, Neer R, Parfitt AM, Whedon GD. Calcium nutrition and bone health in the elderly. Am J Clin Nutr. 1982;36(suppl 5):986-1013.

21. Heany RP, Recker RR, Stegman MR, Moy AJ. Calcium absorption in women: relationships to calcium intake, estrogen status and age. J Bone Miner Res. 1989;4:469-475.

22. Avioli LB. Diseases of bone: calcium, phosphorous and bone metabolism. In: Beeson PB, McDermott W, Wyngaarden JB, eds. Cecil Textbook of Medicine. Philadelphia: WB Saunders and Co; 1979:2225-2231.

23. Sheikh MS. Santa Ana CA, Nicar MJ, Schiller LR, Fordtran JS. Gastrointestinal absorption of calcium from milk and calcium salts. N Engl J Med. 1987;317:532-536.

24. Nicar MJ, Pak CY. Calcium availability from calcium carbonate and calcium citrate. J Clin Endocrinol Metab. 1985;61:391-393.
25. Carr CJ, Shangraw RF. Nutritional and pharmaceutical aspects of calcium supplementation. Am Pharm. 1987;NS27:49-50, 54-57.
26. Parfitt AM. Integration of skeletal and mineral homeostasis. In: DeLuca HF, Frost H, Jee W, Johnston C, Parfitt AM, eds. Osteoporosis: Recent Advances in Pathogenesis and Treatment. Baltimore: University Park Press; 1981:115-126.
27. Harvey JA, Zobita MM, Pak CY. Calcium citrate: reduced propensity for the crystallization of calcium oxalate in urine resulting from induced hypercalciuria of calcium supplementation. J Clin Endocrinol Metab. 1985;61:1223-1225.
28. Holbrook TL, Barrett-Connor E, Wingard DL. Dietary calcium and the risk of hip fracture: 14 year prospective population study. Lancet. 1988;2:1046-1049.
29. Kelly PJ, Pocock Na, Sambrook PN, Eisman JA. Dietary calcium, sex hormones and bone mineral density in normal men. Br Med J. 1990;300:1261-1264.
30. Heaney RP, Davies KM, Ricker RR, Packard PT. Long term consistency of nutrient intakes in humans. J Nutr. 1990;120:869-875.
31. Notelovitch, M. Osteoporosis: screening, prevention and management. Fertil and Steril. 1993;59:707-725.
32. Nordin BE, Horsman A, Crilly RG, Marshall DH, Simpson M. Treatment of spinal osteoporosis in postmenopausal women. Br Med J. 1980;280:451-455.
33. Marcus R, Cann C. Madvig P, et al. Menstrual function and bone mass in elite women distance runners. Ann Intern Med. 1985;102:158-163.
34. Dalsky GP, Stocke KS, Ehsani AA, Slatopolsky E, Lee WC, Birge SJ. Weight bearing exercise training and lumbar bone mineral content in postmenopausal women. Ann Intern Med. 1988;108:824-828.
35. Orwoll ES, Ferar J, Oviatt SK, McClung MR, Huntington K. The relationship of swimming exercise

to bone mass in men and women. Arch Intern Med. 1989;295:1441-1444.

36. Cavanaugh DJ, Cann CE. Brisk walking does not stop bone loss in postmenopausal women. Bone. 1988;9:201-204.

37. Smith EL, Gilligan C, McAdam M, Ensign CP, Smith PE. Deterring bone loss by exercise intervention in premenopausal and postmenopausal women. Calcif Tissue Int. 1989;44:312-321.

38. Notelovitz M, Martin D, Tesar R, Khan FY, et al. Estrogen therapy and variable-resistance weight training increase bone mineral in surgically menopausal women. J Bone Miner Res. 1991;6:583-590.

39. Lindsay R, Tohme JF. Estrogen treatment of patients with established postmenopausal osteoporosis. Obstet Gynecol. 1990;76:290-295.

40. Jilka RL, Hango G, Girasole G, et al. Increased osteoclast development after estrogen loss: mediation by interleukin 6. Science. 1992;257:88-91.

41. Christiansen C, Lindsay R. Estrogens, bone loss and preservation. Osteoporos Int. 1990;1:7-13.

42. Lindsay R, Hart DM, Clark DM. The minimum effective dose of estrogen for prevention of postmenopausal bone loss. Obstet Gynecol. 1984;63:759-763.

43. Horsman A, Jones M, Francis R, Nordin C. The effect of estrogen dose on postmenopausal bone loss. N Engl J Med. 1983;309:1405-1407.

44. De Cree C, Lewin R, Ostyn M. Suitability of cyproterone acetate in the treatment of osteoporosis associated with athletic amenorrhea. Int J Sports Med. 1988;9:187-192.

45. Dupont WD, Page DL. Menopausal estrogen replacement therapy and breast cancer. Arch Intern Med. 1991;51:67-72.

46. Stevenson JC, Cust MP, Gangar KF, Hillard TC, Lees B, Whitehead MI. Effects of transdermal versus oral hormone replacement therapy on bone density in spine and proximal femur in postmenopausal women. Lancet. 1990;335:265-269.

47. Munk-Jensen N, Pors Nielsen S, Obel EB, Bonne-Ericksen P. Reversal of postmenopausal vertebral bone loss by oestrogen and progestogen: a double blind placebo controlled study. Br Med J. 1988;296:1150-1152.
48. Ettinger B, Genant HK, Can CE. Low-dosage estrogen combined with calcium prevents postmenopausal bone loss: results of a three year study. In: Cohn DV, Martin TJ, Meuniere PJ, eds. Calcium Regulation and Bone Metabolism: Basic and Clinical Aspects. Amsterdam: Elsevier; 1987:918-922.
49. Alden JC. Osteoporosis: a review. Clin Ther. 1989;11:3-14.
50. Raisz, LG. Reported at the 1994 meeting of the North American Menopause Society.
51. MacIntyre I, Stevenson J, Whitehead M, Wimalawansa S, Banks L, Healy M. Calcitonin for prevention of postmenopausal bone loss. Lancet. 1988;1:990-992.
52. Reginster J, Albert A, Lecart M, Lambelin P, Denis D, Deroisy R, Fontaine M, Franchimont P. One-year controlled randomized trial of prevention of early postmenopausal bone loss by intranasal calcitonin. Lancet. 1987;1481-1493.
53. Peck W, Riggs BL, Bell N, Wallance R, Johnston C. Gordon S, Shulman L. Research directions in osteoporosis. Am J Med. 1988;84:275-282.
54. Riggs B, Hodgson S, O'Fallon M, Chao C, Wahner H, Muhs J, Cedel S, Melton J. Effects of fluoride treatment on the fracture rate in postmenopausal women with osteoporosis. N Engl J Med. 1990;322:802-809.
55. Zerwekh JE, Antich P, Sakhaee K, Gonzales J, Pak CY. Intermittent slow-release sodium fluoride therapy produces "stronger bone" at the microscopic level. J Bone Min Res. 1989;4:998A.
56. Watts N, Harris S, Genant H, Wasnich R, Miller P, Jackson R, Licata A, Ross P, Woodson G, Yanover M, Mysiu J, Kohse L, Rao M, Steiger P, Richmond B, Chestnut C. Intermittent cyclical etidronate treatment of postmenopausal osteoporosis. N Engl J Med. 1990;323:73-79.

57. Storm T, Thomsborg G, Steiniche T, Genant H, Sorensen O. Effect of intermittent cyclical etidronate therapy on bone mass and fracture rate in women with postmenopausal osteoporosis. N Engl J Med. 1990;322:1265-1271.
58. Ettinger B, Genant KH, Cann CE. Long-term estrogen replacement therapy prevents bone loss and fractures. Ann Int Med. 1985;102:319-324.

Chapter 2

The Brain

There are significant differences in the way mammals behave that reflect gender-specific differences in brain function. Some of these are obvious, such as the complimentary, complex elaborate patterns of mating behavior in some species. Some are not obvious at all and bear witness to the surprisingly abundant gender-specific differences in the central nervous system (CNS). In general, these only become important when the same tests of function are applied to men and women without taking the sex of the subject into account. An example of this is the auditory brainstem response which has a longer latency period and smaller amplitude in men than in women.[1] Head size (larger in men) accounts for only 50% of the observed differences between the sexes; normal young women, moreover, have no less than five reproducible and significant changes in the duration of the latent period during monthly hormonal cycling.

Several investigators have described sex-specific behavioral traits or abilities. Males are alleged to have superior ability for mathematical reasoning,[2,3] while women are said to be better at pain discrimination.[4] Linn and Petersen have concluded that from childhood to adulthood, males are faster at solving problems involving some

19

types of spatial perceptions than are women[5] and Robert and Tanguay have shown in a careful study that these differences persist into old age.[6] Whether or not these differences in cognitive ability are learned behaviors or a consequence of significant differences in brain anatomy and molecular biology between the sexes is difficult to establish. In fact, more recent research showed that differences in visual spatial ability and verbal ability between the sexes did not account for more than 1-5% of the group variance.[7] Cognitive function in the sexes can vary at certain ages in some respects but compared across most age ranges, differences in general intellectual ability and IQ scores are minimal.[8] The alleged preponderance of learning disabilities in males (ranging from 3:1 to 15:1) may be, in part, a consequence of the fact that most literature on learning disabilities concentrates on male subjects.[9]

There is no question, however, that significant gender-specific differences exist in both the anatomy and in the chemistry of neural transmission in the CNS. These unique features appear early in fetal life and are, in large part, due to the organizing action of hormones secreted by the gonads, thyroid and adrenal glands on the developing brain. Sexually dimorphic neuronal connections are not restricted to the hypothalamus (which regulates reproductive behavior and gonadotropin secretion), but are found throughout the brain.[10] Pilgrim and Reisert suggest that neurological (chorea minor, migraine headaches) and psychiatric diseases (depression) that are more common in one sex (women in each of these three cases) are actually the consequences of neurodevelopmental errors.

The Role of Estrogen in Differentiation and Maintenance of the Brain

Estrogen plays a pivotally important role in the differentiation of the brain. It is responsible for the sexual dimorphism of many portions of the brain and produces significant differences in neuronal number, structure and function.[11] The trophic action of gonadal steroid is believed to be responsible for gender-specific differences in cognitive function, memory and learning behavior, among others.[12-16] Interestingly, in fetal life it is not principally the circulating estrogen that effects CNS differentiation and development; the fetus is protected from the high levels of maternal estrogen by equally high levels of a circulating fetoprotein that binds the hormone. Rather, the estrogen responsible for neuronal proliferation and differentiation during fetal life is almost exclusively that produced intraneuronally by the conversion of circulating androgens to estradiol by the enzyme aromatase, which is distributed throughout the entire neuron.[17]

The receptor for estrogen is a nuclear transcription factor. In the presence of the hormone it activates target genes to begin a cascade of poorly understood interactions that are essential to the differentiation of the developing mammalian brain.[18a,18b] Whether or not estrogen acts relatively directly to effect neuronal differentiation or through interactions with locally synthesized neurotrophins such as nerve growth factor is incompletely understood. Torran-Allerand has suggested, however, that the widespread and highly specialized effects of estrogen not only in the brain but throughout the body are best explained by its interaction with both tissue and developmental stage-specific growth factors.[19,20] This idea explains the varied effects of estrogen on many tissues as well as at various stages of life.

Estrogen receptors are present throughout fetal as well as adult life in many areas of the developing hypothalamus, preoptic area, hippocampus and basal forebrain. In contrast, the cerebral cortex demonstrates these receptors only during developmental life. However, estrogen's presence in adequate amounts ensures the maintenance and repair of neurons in the adult CNS. In cases of neuronal damage or destruction, sensitivity to estrogen is reactivated in the adult CNS. Indeed, Naftolin has demonstrated estrogen-induced synaptic remodeling in adult primates.[21] It is likely that adequate levels of estrogen are necessary for memory storage in the adult, for example, and for learning new tasks, which apparently involves recruiting and modifying a progressively increasing number of neurons in the primary motor and sensory cortex of the brain.[22]

Estrogen deprivation may be responsible for some of the neurodegenerative diseases of aging. Several studies suggest that this is in fact the case, and that gonadal steroid deficiency has a profound effect on cognitive function.[23,24] Estrogen replacement therapy lowers the risk of Alzheimer's disease by 40% in females. This disorder is twice as prevalent in women as in men, a skewing not observed in other dementias. Toran-Allerand cautions that using estrogen antagonists like tamoxifen over a long period of time may compromise a patient's ability to maintain optimal neuronal numbers and/or function. She urges longitudinal studies of cognitive ability in women who are deprived of estrogen's effect, whether because of postmenopausal age, tamoxifen administration or oophorectomy.[25]

Testosterone has a direct differentiating effect on the brain during development in a few specific areas: the behavioral trait of aggression, as evidenced in the play behavior of boys, is an example of one of them. The bulk of the impact of testosterone on brain differentiation, though, is through intraneuronal conversion by aromatase to estrogen.

Gender-Specific Differences in Brain Structure and Function

The gross volume of the brain as well as neuronal anatomy are dimorphic; differences are most pronounced in some of the areas of the brain postulated to be responsible for mood and behavior.[26] Among the best established differences are the dimorphism of the sexually dimorphic nucleus in the preoptic hypothalamus (larger in males),[27] the suprachiasmatic nucleus of the hypothalamus, (important for circadian rhythms, which are disturbed in depression)[28] and the cerebral cortex.[29] The gonadal steroids influence the asymmetry of the cerebrum: portions of the left hemisphere are more prominent in males. Some investigators correlate this with a reported greater hemispheric specialization at earlier ages in males and the lower incidence in females of developmental disorders associated with language deficits (known to be associated with the left hemisphere).[30] Others relate the relative protection of women from schizophrenia to estrogen's downregulation of D2 (dopamine) receptors in the striatum.[31,32] This notion of estrogen's moderating effect on schizophrenia is reinforced by the clinical observations of the increased rate of schizophrenic relapses in women premenstrually, postpartum and after menopause, as well as remission during pregnancy.

Women and Depression

Women are two to three times more likely to experience depression than are men.[33] The gender difference emerges in midadolescence at about the age of 15. Some, like Barnett, attribute most if not all of this increased vulnerability to societally imposed gender role definitions that allow women less independence and autonomy than men.[34] In a provocative review, Halbriech and Lumley speculate that gonadal hormones' influence on neuronal anatomy and function may be related to the increased incidence of depression in women compared with that in men.[35] They summarize the important findings concerning the complex relationship between neurotransmitters and depression, pointing out that adrenergic, cholinergic, dopaminergic and serotonin systems are all implicated in the genesis of the disorder. The multiplicity of interactions between these neuronal systems may explain the clinical observation that any one of several different antidepressants may be effective in the same patient, although one or two might work better than the rest.

In an effort to correlate gender-specific differences in levels of neurotransmitters with the higher incidence of depression in women, Halbreich and Lumley demonstrated differences in 3-methoxy-4-hydroxyphenylglycol (MHPG), the main metabolite of norepinephrine, which increases

with age in both normal men and women but is significantly higher for women. The sex difference persisted in
endogenously depressed women and men, but in addition,
had a different pattern in the two sexes. Depresssed women
were separated into two groups: those with higher than
normal MHPG and those with lower than normal MHPG for
their age. In endogenously depressed men, only a higher
than normal MHPG or normal level per age group could be
demonstrated. Of note is the fact that estradiol may inhibit
norepinephrine uptake.[36]

There are gender-specific differences in the serotoninergic system (5-HT) in various parts of the brain, including
the hypothalamus, that can be influenced by hormonal
manipulation.[37]

A subtype of premenstrual tension (late luteal phase
dysphoric disorder) in women may be explained by serotonin system dysregulation.[38] The 5-HT system ages (as evidenced by the degree of imipramine binding) more intense-
ly in women than in men, and 5-HT reuptake inhibitors
may be particularly useful in treating depression in older
females.[39]

Arguing against the notion that gender-specific differences in the biochemistry of neural tissue are responsible
for the prevalence of depression in women is the meticulous epidemiological work of Kessler and his colleagues.[40]
They point out that the higher rate of depression in women
is almost exclusively related to the greater risk of women
for a first onset of a 12-month depression; they found no
difference in the rates of chronic depression or recurrences
of depression between males and females.

Murphy, reviewing reports from four longitudinal
studies on depression, comments that although depression
and anxiety were more frequent in women at the century's
midpoint, by the end of the third quarter, the occurrence
had become more equal between the sexes. The author con-
cludes that the phenomenon is real and probably related to
changing roles for men and women.[41]

In fact, the available data suggest that depression is a
complex disorder and probably involves interaction between
genetic, hormonal, situational and other influences.

In their review, Reisert and Pilgrim point out that in addition to depression, several other neurological and affective disorders predominate in women, among them, chorea minor, tardive dyskinesia, infantile hyperkinetic syndrome and migraine.[10] They suggest that attention to the mechanisms for the generation of sexual dimorphisms in the brain might result in better techniques for preventing and treating these diseases. While they agree that there is a critical period in differentiation (which might be different for different areas of the CNS) in which estrogen plays a crucial role, they point out that some sex-specific differences in the brain are not hormonally mediated but are probably under primary genetic control. Using gender-specific cell cultures of embryonic brainstem, they showed that there were region-specific morphological (male neurons were about a third larger than female neurons) and functional (female and male neurons took up significantly different amounts of dopamine in both diencephalic and mesencephalic cultures) sex differences in dopaminergic neurons. The phenomena were not an artifact of the culture method: serotoninergic neurons showed no such gender-specific differences.

Some of the traditional laboratory testing for depression must be individualized for men and women. Schittecate and his colleagues have shown, for example, that the well-known blunted response of growth hormone levels to intravenous clonidine in depressed patients (which has been proposed as a biological marker of primary major depression) is different in men and women.[42] While the test discriminated between major and minor depression in men, it did not do so in women. Furthermore, if women were post-menopausal, their response was significantly less pronounced than that of women who were still menstruating.

Depression and Cyclic Hormonal Fluctuations in Women

The impact of hormonal fluctuations on mood in some women is evident, most strikingly in those who experience postpartum depression (two women in every 1,000 who give birth) and in those who experience some variation of premenstrual dysphoria (estimated to be about 20% of menstruating females). The belief that emotionally healthy women experience clinically significant depression after hysterectomy or "involutional melancholia," the onset of depression with menopause, has faded.[43]

Pedersen and his group summarized hormonal variations during the peripartum period, pointing out that patients with histories of depression had blunted responses to thyroid stimulating hormone (TSH) as well as elevated serum and urinary cortisol which did not suppress with dexamethasone. The data suggest a preexisting, blunted hypothalamic pituitary axis response to feedback from the thyroid and adrenal glands, which the authors felt might have been unmasked by the stress of the peripartum period. They termed the imbalance a consequence of "an endocrine scar". They also described significantly lower thyroid hormone levels in women with postpartum dysphoria, and postulated that the depressed patient might have had a deficiency of thyroid hormone in the brain, partially due to the elevated levels of thyroid-binding globulin that are characteristic of pregnancy.[44] In addition, women who were depressed after delivery seemed to have an elevated morning serum cortisol, although their 24 hour free cortisol excretion was normal, suggesting a disturbance of the normal diurnal cycle.

The American Psychiatric Association has recently defined a subset of women with premenstrual syndrome who experience a syndrome now called Premenstrual Dysphoric Disorder (PMDD) that begins 3-10 days before the menstrual period and lasts until the first few days of menses have passed.[45] They may have no other mental or physical disorder, and represent about 3-8% of premenopausal women. Symptoms do not resemble those of classic endogenous depression, but are more likely to be associated with hypersomnia, increased appetite, anxiety and irritability.[46]

The Use of Antidepressants in Women

Several issues are important for women who take antidepressants.[47] Fluoxetine produces anorgasmia in women and difficulty achieving climax and ejaculation in men. Buproprion, which combats anxiety, may induce seizures in anorexic patients. There are important differences in the metabolism of tricyclic antidepressants; women over age 50 or women who are on oral contraceptives require lower doses, while higher doses are required premenstrually for women who become symptomatic at that time.[48]

Some antidepressant drugs are contraindicated in pregnant women; MAO inhibitors are teratogenic in animals and may also precipitate hypertensive crises, particularly if dietary restrictions are not scrupulously observed. Anticholinergic effects of tricyclic antidepressants can cause tachyarrhythmias in the fetus and newborns may have withdrawal syndromes characterized by tachypnea, fast heart rates and irritability. Careful tapering of the drug 2 to 3 weeks before the expected delivery date may avoid withdrawl syndrome in the infant. Due to the fluid shifts that characterize pregnancy, physicians should choose antidepressants that have serum concentrations that are easy to measure.[49]

Finally, many pregnant women are reluctant to take any medication during pregnancy and may refuse to continue antidepressants during the gravid state; such women may require special psychotherapy during this vulnerable period.

References

1. Dehan CP, Jerger J. Analysis of gender differences in the auditory brainstem response. Laryngoscope. 1990;100: 18-24.
2. Benbow CP. Sex differences in mathematical reasoning ability in intellectually talented preadolescents: their

nature, effects and possible causes. Behav Brain Sci. 1988;11:169-232.

3. Kerns KA, Berenbaum SA. Sex differences in spatial ability in children. Behav Genet. 1991;21:383-396.

4. Feine JS, Bushnell MC, Miron D, Duncan GH. Sex differences ' the perception of noxious heat stimuli. Pain. 199 ,44:255-262.

5. Linn MC, Petersen AC. Emergence and characterization of sex differences in spatial ability: a meta-analysis. Child Dev. 1985;56:1479-1498.

6. Robert M, Tanguay M. Perception and representation of the Euclidean coordinates in mature and elderly men and women. Exp Aging Res. 1990;16:123-131.

7. Vogel SA. Gender differences in intelligence, language, visual-motor abilities and academic achievement in students with learning disabilities: a review of the literature. J Learn Disabil. 1990;23:44-52.

8. Denno D, Myers B, Nachson I. Early cognitive functioning: sex and race differences. Int J Neurosci. 1982;16:159-172.

9. Finucc JM, Childs B. Are there really more dyslexic boys than girls? In: Ansara A, Geschwind N, Galaburda A, Albert M, Gartreell N, eds. Sex Differences in Dyslexia. Baltimore: Orton Dyslexia Society; 1981:1-10.

10. Pilgrim C, Reisert I. Differences between male and female brains: developmental mechanisms and implications. Horm Metab Res. 1992;24:353-359.

11. Toran-Allerand CD. Organotypic culture of the developing cerebral cortex and hypothalamus: relevance to sexual differentiation. Psychoneuroendocrinology. 1991;16:7-24.

12. Toran-Allerand CD. On the genesis of sexual differentiation of the general nervous system: morphogenetic consequences of steroidal exposure and possible role of alpha-fetoprotein. Prog Brain Res. 1984;61:63-98.

13. Nishizuka N, Arai Y. Sexual dimorphism in synaptic organization in the amygdala and its dependence on neonatal hormone environment. Brain Res. 1981;212:31-38.

14. Stanley HF, Borthwick NM, Fink G. Brain protein changes during development and sexual differentiation in the rat. Brain Res. 1986;370:215-222.

15. Stanley HF, Fink G. Synthesis of specific brain proteins is influenced by testosterone at mRNA level in the neonatal rat. Brain Res. 1986;370:223-231.

16. Hammer RP, Jacobson CD. Sex difference in dendritic development of the sexually dimorphic nucleus of the preoptic area in the rat. Int J Dev Neurosci. 1984;2:77-85.

17. Naftolin F, Ryan KJ, Davies I, et al. The formation of estrogens by central neuroendocrine tissues. Recent Progr Horm Res. 1975;31:295.

18a. Evans RM. The steroid and thyroid hormone receptor superfamily. Science. 1988;240:889-895.

18b. Beato M. Gene regulation by steroid hormones. Cell. 1989;56:335-344.

19. Sohrabji F, Green LA, Miranda RC, Toran-Allerand, CD. Reciprocal regulation of estrogen and NGF receptors by their ligands in PC12 cells. J Neurobiol. 1994;25:974-988.

20. Sohrabji F, Miranda RC, Toran-Allerand CD. Estrogen differentially regulates estrogen and nerve growth factor receptor mRNAs in adult sensory neurons. J Neurosci. 1994;412:459-471.

21. Naftolin F, Leranth C, Perez J, et al. Estrogen induces synaptic plasticity in adult primate neurons. Neuroendocrinology. 1993;57:935-939.

22. Barinaga M. Watching the brain remake itself. Science. Dec 2, 1994;266:1475-1476.

23. Hier DB, Crowley WF Jr. Spatial ability in androgen deficient men. N Engl J Med. 1982;306:1202-1205.

24. Gabrieli JD, Corkin S, Crawford JD. The influence of sex steroids on human nonverbal memory processes. Ann NY Acad Sci. 1985;444:457-459.

25. Toran-Allerand D. Personal communication. August, 1994.

26. Goy RW, McEwen BS. Sexual Differentiation of the Brain. Based on a work session of the neuroscience research program. Cambridge, MA: MIT Press; 1980;12.

27. Arnold AP, Gorski RA. Gonadal steroid induction of structural sex differences in the central nervous system. Annu Rev Neursci. 1984;7:413-442.
28. Swaab DF, Hoffman MA. Sexual differentiation of the human brain: a historical perspective. Prog Brain Res. 1984;61:361-374.
29. Diamond MC. Hormonal effects on the development of cerebral lateralization. Psychoneuroendocrinology. 1991;16:121-129.
30. Kelly DD. Sexual differentiation of the nervous system. In: Kandel ER, Schwartz JH, Jessell TM, eds. Principles of Neuronal Science. 3rd ed. New York: Elsevier; 1991.
31. Roy EJ, Buyer DR, Licari VA. Estradiol in the striatum; effects on behavior and dopamine receptors but no evidence for membrane steroid receptors. Brain Res Bull. 1990;25:221-227.
32. Hafner H, Behrens S, DeVry J, Gattaz WF. An animal model for the effects of estradiol on dopamine mediated behavior: implications for sex differences in schizophrenia. Psychiatry Res. 1991;38:125-134.
33. Weissman MM, Klerman GL. Sex differences in the epidemiology of depression. Arch Gen Psychiatry. 1977;34.98-111.
34. Barnett RC, Baruch KG. Social roles, gender and psychological distress. In: Barnett RC, Bierner L, Baruch GK, eds. Gender and Stress. New York: The Free Press; 1987:122-143.
35. Halbreich U, Lumley LA. The multiple interactional biological processes that might lead to depression and gender differences in its appearance. J of Affect Disord. 1993;29:159-173.
36. Best NR, Rees MP, Barlow DH, Cowen PH. Effect of estradiol implant on noradrenergic function and mood in menopausal subjects. Psychoneuroendocrinology. 1992;17:87-93.
37. Biegon A, Reches A, Snyder L, McEwen BS. Serotonergic and noradrenergic receptors in the rat brain: modulation by chronic exposure to ovarian hormones. Life Sci. 1983;32:2015-2021.

38. Lepage P, Steiner M. Gender and serotonergic dysregulation: implications for late luteal phase dysphoric disorder. In: Cassano GB, Akiskal HS, eds. Royal Society of Medicine Services International Congress and Symposium Series No. 165. Royal Society of Medicine Services Limited; 1991:131-143.
39. Doogan DP, Caillard V. Sertraline in the prevention of depression. Br J Psychiatry. 1992;160:127-222.
40. Kessler RC, McGonage KA, Swartz MS, Blazer DG, Nelson CB. Sex and depression in the National Comorbidity Survey I: lifetime prevalence, chronicity and recurrence. J Affect Disord. 1993;29:85-96.
41. Murphy JM. Trends in depression and anxiety: men and women. Acta Psychiatr Scand. 1986;73:113-127.
42. Schittecate M, Charles G, Machowski R, Dumont F, Garcia-Valentin J, Wilmotte J, Papart P, Pitchot W, Wauthy J, Ansseau M, Hoffmann G, Pelc I. Effects of gender and diagnosis on growth hormone response to clonidine for major depression: a large-scale multicenter study. Am J Psychiatry 1994;151:216-220.
43. Gitlin MJ, Pasnau RO. Psychiatric syndromes linked to reproductive functioning women: a review of current knowledge. Am J Psychiatry 1989;146:1413-1422.
44. Williams RH. Textbook of Endocrinology. 60th ed. Philadelphia: W.B. Saunders Co; 1985.
45. Diagnostic and Statistical Manual. American Psychiatric Association. 4th ed. 1994.
46. Halbreich U, Endicott J. Relationship of dysphoric premenstrual changes to depressive disorders. Acta Psychiatr Scand. 1985;71:331-338.
47. Coyne JC, Schwenk TL. Depression in the female patient. The Female Patient. 1994;19:45-57.
48. Hamilton JA, Halbreich U. Special aspects of neuropsychiatric illnesses in women: with a focus on depression. Annu Rev Med. 1993;44:355-364.
49. Miller LJ. Clinical strategies for the use of psychotropic drugs during pregnancy. Psychiatric Med 1991;9:275-298.

Chapter 3

The Breast

After lung cancer, breast cancer kills more women than any other malignancy. The rate of breast cancer has been increasing steadily in the United States over the past 40 years[1] and women are convinced that this malignancy is epidemic.

Many epidemiologists believe that females are paying for earlier maturation, as nutrition in developed countries improves, with an increased risk for developing breast cancer.[2-5] This is particularly true if menarche occurs before the age of 13, and of taller women, both Western and Japanese.[2]

Cancer: A Disorder of Normal Growth and Differentiation

A fascinating current view of the pathogenesis of cancer is that it is the consequence of a (possibly systemic) failure of growth control in the afflicted patient. James Devitt, who reviewed the basis for this belief and speculated about the implications for cancer of the breast,[6] advances the notion that the course of this malignancy in the host is determined importantly (if not exclusively) by the local organ-tissue factors that regulate growth. He explains that this is the reason patients fare quite differently with the same initial lesion, regardless of what therapeutic regimen is mounted to save them.

Several families of growth factors (and their membrane receptors) are present in both normal and malignant tissue. Interaction between various growth factors (i.e., epidermal growth factor, transforming growth factor alpha, HER2/neu oncoprotein, insulin and insulin-like growth factor and fibroblast growth factors) and their receptors on the cell membrane enables both intra- and intercellular changes which affect tissue growth and differentiation. Such changes are responsible for the proliferative, invasive and metastatic characteristics of any individual cancer.[7] The newest anticancer regimens focus on how to identify these receptors on cancer cells and detect which growth factors in their environment are influencing their malignant properties.

The sequence after binding of a growth factor to a cell membrane receptor is incompletely and probably partially inaccurately understood, but involves a complex series of second messengers and the induction of "immediate early response" genes in the cell such as c-myc, c-fos and c-jun.[8] The results of the process vary depending on the type of cell, which of its receptors is being targeted, and the environment in which it exists; growth inhibition, for example, is a possible result of the process.

Estrogen binding by breast cancer cells was one of the first examples of the impact of a ligand on the characteristics of the resulting tumor: it stimulated the growth of cancers populated by cells with estrogen receptors.[9] This observation is the rationale for the success of tamoxifen (an estrogen analogue) therapy of estrogen-receptor-positive breast cancer.[10] However, a recent finding that tamoxifen therapy induced endometrial cancer of a particularly malignant type in women included in the Breast Cancer Prevention Trial sponsored by the National Cancer Institute (principal investigator Bernard Fisher) is prompting a second look at this agent as a viable treatment for estrogen-receptor positive cancer of the breast.[11]

Other approaches are currently being pursued in the treatment of breast cancer. They are all based on the model of breast cancer as essentially the result of the dysregulation of normal mechanisms that ensure tissue maintenance and repair. They include stategies directed at the following:

- epidermal growth factor receptor and its ligand. These include antiepidermal growth factor receptor antibody,[12] the microinjection of EGF-R antisense RNA,[13] or antisense transforming growth factor alpha mRNA[14] into EGF-R overexpressing cells.
- amphiregulin, another member of the epidermal growth factor family that was initially detected in a breast cancer cell line and which inhibits rather than stimulates growth.[15]
- monocolonal anti-p[185] antibody directed at the HER2/neu oncogene product p[185] (which is identical to epidermal growth factor receptor). P[185] is normally expressed primarily in developing and adult neural tissue.[16,17] It may not only block this receptor, but may actually inhibit tumor growth.[18] Because cancers that express HER2/neu seem particularly sensitive to chemotherapy, strategies that combine antibodies to the oncogene with chemotherapy may be more useful than chemotherapy alone.

There seems to be a whole family of p[185] ligands and their action may vary; under some conditions, the ligand actually induces differentiation of cultured human breast cancer cells.[19]

- Antifibroblast growth factor antibodies attack a family of receptors that require binding to heparin for functionality.[20] The fibroblast growth factor apparently promotes angiogenesis as well as cell proliferation, so inactivating the cell's FGF receptor might attack the cancer by two separate mechanisms.
- Blocking the receptor to platelet-derived growth factor on neoplastic cells may or may not turn out to be useful in

combatting breast cancer. Elevated plasma PDGF levels are seen in some patients with advanced, metastatic breast cancer.[21]

- Dysregulation of the role of insulin and insulin-like growth factors (the somatomedins) may contribute to breast cancer: they and their receptors appear to regulate normal cellular growth and metabolism. Peptide analogues to insulin have been created that inhibit a variety of cancer cell lines in vitro.

- Somatostatin, a hypothalamic tetrapeptide that suppresses lactogenic hormones, growth hormone and prolactin, also inhibits the growth breast cancer cells as well as angiogenesis.[22,23]

- Several growth-inhibitory factors and receptors are being investigated for their effectiveness in treating cancer. The prototype is transforming growth factor beta; these growth-inhibitory peptides appear during embryogenesis and are involved in tissue regression during differentiation. Localized delivery of these factors to tumors may be necessary; nontargeted administration in mice produced organ fibrosis and cachexia.[24]

- Compounds that are nonspecific growth factor antagonists are also being tried: suramin, putrescine, spermidine and spermine are all examples of these.

Another obvious target of antineoplastic therapy will be to find compounds that interfere with the second messengers set off by receptor-ligand impact on the cell. Similarly, introducing genes encoding for mutant Fos or Jun proteins into malignant cells is another strategy that is being considered for development.

Recently, scientists have been working out the steps in the fascinating sequence of how a cell is prompted to specialize and, *pari passu,* lose its ability to divide. Both the stimulus to specialize and to stop division seem to come from the same group of key cell cycle enzymes, the cyclin-dependent kinases (cdk) which by phosphorylating other cell proteins, inactivate them. One of these inhibitors is p21, a cdk inhibitor in muscle cells.[25] Interestingly, as muscle cells (in which most of the classic work has been done) begin to differentiate and produce specialized proteins like myosin, they produce a family of proteins called the myogenic basic helix-loop-helix proteins; these "turn on" the genes that make tissue specific proteins and at the same time, turn on the p21 gene, which, it is postulated, makes further cell division impossible. Other scientists, as well as these, have found that p21 turns on at the end stage of cell differentiation in other tissues; these include cartilage, skin and the mucosal lining of the nose. The data need further refinement and investigation, but a whole family of proteins that make cell division impossible have been identified. Further therapy for cancer may include substances that induce the production of such cdk phosphorylators.

The Breast Cancer Gene

Of women suffering from breast cancer, 5-20% have a positive family history of the disease. A small subset, however, seem to be representative of families with a high degree of penetrance of a gene that predisposes them to the malignancy; it is in these women that the **BRCA1**[26] and **BRCA2**[27] genes were recently identified. Female patients who have a mutation in these genes may develop breast malignancies; those who have a hazardous mutation of the **BRCA1** gene will develop the cancer when they are less than 45 years of age.[28] About 5% of breast cancers are thought to result from mutations in the **BRCA1** gene.

A confounding issue with the new-found gene is that its discoverers have found it capable of many mutations,[29] so that screening women for a hazardous defect will not be a trivial task. The most likely women to have a dangerous mutation in their **BRCA1** gene are those with a family history of two members with breast and two with ovarian cancer; **BRCA1** mutations are harder to identify in families who only have multiple cases of breast cancer but no ovarian malignancy. So far, whether mutations in **BRCA1** have any relationship to sporadic breast cancer (i.e., without a suggestive family history) is unknown.

In a recent short communication in Lancet,[30] Easton and his colleagues listed the known facts about the **BRCA** gene. They are:

—Mutations of **BRCA1** account for over 80% of families with multiple cases of early onset breast cancer plus ovarian cancer or multiple cases of ovarian cancer without breast cancer. Only a minority of families with early onset breast cancer but no ovarian cancer seem to be linked to **BRCA1**.

—Only invasive epithelial ovarian cancers have been shown to occur in **BRCA1** families. There is no evidence that borderline or nonepithelial tumors are caused by **BRCA1**.

—Breast cancer in males is occasionally hereditary but does not seem to be a characteristic of **BRCA1** families.[31]

—**BRCA1** mutations confer a risk of 51% by age 50, and 85% by age 70, for breast cancer. For ovarian cancer, the figures are 23% by age 50, and 63% by age 70.

—Women in **BRCA1** families with breast cancer are at high risk of both a second primary breast cancer and of ovarian cancer.

—**BRCA1** mutant families are at increased risk of prostate cancer and, in both men and women, of colon cancer.

—The proportion of individuals in the general population who carry **BRCA1** mutations is between 1 in 500 and 1 in 2,000. The proportion of the population that carries a mutation in any of the breast cancer genes is much higher.

Hormones and Cancer of the Breast

Oral Contraceptives

A recent study done in the Netherlands is of interest because of the large number of women studied (over 900) and the fact that the proportion of women using oral contraceptives in the Netherlands is among the largest in the world.[32] Overall, long-term use of oral contraceptives (i.e., longer than 12 years) produces a relative risk (RR) of 1.3 in women for breast cancer. The relative risk changes with the ages of patients using the medication. The hazard is greatest for women who begin before 20: RR increases 1.44 per year of early use. If women use oral contraceptives before age 36, RR is 2.1, and after age 45, 1.9. Four or more years of oral contraceptive use, particularly for women under 20 years of age, increases relative risk for breast cancer. For women between the ages of 36 and 45, however, duration of use had no impact on the relative risk of developing breast cancer. Meta-analyses have confirmed the notion that longer term use of oral contraceptives increases the risk of early breast cancer.[33-35.]

Depot medroxyprogesterone acetate, now approved for long-term contraception by the FDA, is thought by some investigators to increase the risk of breast cancer; the first data came from studies on beagles.[36]

Two epidemiological studies in humans[37,38] were reassuring enough to prompt FDA approval of the contraceptive, but a pooled analysis of data from both studies showed an increased risk of breast cancer observed in recent or current users of the agent.[39]

Hormonal Replacement Therapy in the Postmenopausal Patient

One of the most compelling and interesting issues in treating women who have survived breast cancer is whether or not to encourage them to use postmenopausal estrogen replacement therapy (ERT). Cobleigh and colleagues report that there is no convincing evidence that ERT has any impact on the survival of breast cancer patients, either positively or negatively.[40] The Nurses' Study, on the other hand, found that there was a significant increase in the relative risk for breast cancer in women currently using estrogen alone (RR 1.21) or estrogen plus progestin (RR 1.41). The risk for breast cancer in women who had used hormones for longer than 5 years was greater among older women (RR 1.71).[40a]

Breast Cancer and Diet

Several foods have an apparent impact on whether or not a patient develops cancer of the breast. The role of others is controversial.

Fiber reduces breast cancer incidence in rodents.[41] To date, only observational studies have been done in humans examining the role of ingested substances and their impact on breast cancer, i.e. studies in which women report their intake of certain foods, either retrospectively or prospectively, and the data are correlated with their incidence of breast cancer. One such study is the Nurses' Health Study, in which 121,700 female registered nurses, ages 30 to 55, completed a mailed questionnaire on known and suspected risk factors for cancer and cardiovascular disease. The study began in 1976.[42,43] Every two years since, follow-up questionnaires have been sent, and in 1980 dietary questions were included for the first time.

The Nurses' Study found that dietary fiber afforded some modest protection for middle-aged women from breast cancer over an 8-year period. This may or may not be related to the fact that diets high in fiber may reduce intestinal reabsorption of estrogen excreted via the biliary system.[44] The study did not demonstrate any positive association between intake of either total or specific types of **fat** on the incidence of breast cancer in women, no matter what their menopausal status. In contrast, total and animal fat intake correlated positively with the risk of colon cancer in the same group of women.[45] The general belief that high fat intake bore a relationship to cancer was not, therefore, supported by this study. The authors postulated that the real reason fat restriction might seem to reduce the incidence of breast cancer was in fact the consequence of relatively poor general nutrition, which resulted in shorter adult stature (see opening paragraphs of this chapter). Another relevant point is that women in the Arctic North and in Mediterranean countries take in approximately 40% of their daily calories in fat and have a lower incidence of breast cancer. The fat is provided from fish and olive oil in the diets of these women and the data suggest that saturated, not unsaturated fats are the culprit. Finally, the phytoestrogens contained in soy beans are thought to offer some protection against breast cancer in that they may block estrogen receptors from the cancer-promoting effects of estrogen.

In spite of many studies, **caffeine's** role (and indeed, any of the methyl xanthines) in promoting breast cancer or even fibrocystic disease of the breast remains controversial.[46]

Women and Malignancy: The Protective Role of Estrogen

Women survive cancer better than men[47]; gender alone was responsible for 12% lower hazard rates in women than in men for cancers of the stomach and lung. With malignant melanoma, women had a 33% greater chance of survival than men. Menarche confers protection against epithelial cancers and sarcomas in girls: hazard rates decreased by 55-65% after the age of 11 years.[48] This is thought to be because of the impact of estrogen as a facilitator of distant metastases: cancers whose prognosis did not depend on their association with distant metastases did not show any better prognosis for women at ages when estrogen production occurred. Bolstering the notion that estrogen is protective in cancers in which distant metastases play an important role in causing fatality, postmenopausal women who developed breast cancer did better if they had received recent hormonal replacement therapy (HRT).[49]

Recent enthusiasm for HRT is so great that a substantial number of practitioners are now urging survivors of breast cancer to accept postmenopausal estrogen replacement to reduce osteoporosis and the incidence of coronary artery disease; breast cancer does not have a poorer prognosis in pregnant or premenopausal women than it does in postmenopausal patients.[50]

References

1. Kelsey JL, Gammon MD. The epidemiology of breast cancer. CA Cancer J Clin. 1991;41:147-165.
2. Byers TE, Williamson DR. Diet, alcohol, body size and prevention of breast cancer. In: Stoll BA, ed. Approaches to Breast Cancer Prevention. Dordrecht, The Netherlands: Kluwer Academic; 1991:113-134.
3. Ewertz M. Risk factors for breast cancer and their prognostic significance. Acta Oncol. 1988;27:733-737.
4. De Waard F, Cornelis JP, Aoki K, Yoshida M. Breast cancer incidence according to weight and height in two cities in the Netherlands and in Aichi Prefecture, Japan. Cancer. 1977;40:1269-1276.
5. Yuasa S, MacMahon B. Lactation and reproductive histories of breast cancer patients in Tokyo, Japan. Bull WHO. 1970;42:195-204.
6. Devitt JE. Breast cancer: have we missed the forest because of the tree? Lancet. 1994;344:732-733.
7. Tripathy D, Benz C. Growth factors and their receptors. Breast Cancer. Hematology/Oncology Clinics of North America. 1994;8:29-50.
8. Majerus PW, Ross TS, Cunningham TW, et al. Recent insights into phosphatidylinositol signaling. Cell. 1990;63:459-465.
9. Li S, Plowman GD, Buckley SD, Shipley GD. Heparin inhibition of autonomous growth implicated amphiregulin as an autocrine growth factor for normal human mammary epithelial cells. J Cell Physiol. 1992;153:103-111.
10. Early Breast Trialists' Collaborative Group. System treatment of early breast cancer by hormonal, cytotoxic or immune therapy. Lancet. 1992;339:1-71.

11. Seachrist L. Restating the risks of tamoxifen. Science. 1994;263:910-911.

12. Bates SE, Valerius EM, Ennis BW, et al. Expression of the transforming growth factor alpha/epidermal growth factor receptor pathway in normal breast epithelial cells. Endocrinology. 1990;126:596-607.

13. Moroni MC, Willingham MC, Beguinot L. EGF-R antisense RNA blocks expression of the epidermal growth factor receptor and suppresses the transforming phenotype of a human carcinoma cell line. J Biol Chem. 1992;267:2714-2722.

14. Kenney N, Saeki T, Kim N, et al. Induction of TGF alpha antisense mRNA partially mediated in vitro growth of estrogen responsive (ER+) and nonresponsive (ER-) human breast cancer cells. Proc Am Assoc Cancer Res. 1992;33:275. Abstract.

15. Plowman GD, Green JM, McDonald VC, et al. The amphiregulin gene encodes a novel epidermal growth factor-related protein with tumor inhibitory activity. Mol Cell Biol. 1990;10:1969-1981.

16. Falls DL, Rosen KM, Corfas G, et al. ARIA, a protein that stimulates acetylcholine receptor synthesis, is a member of the Neu ligand family. Cell. 1993;81:801-815.

17. Orr-Urtreger A, Trakhtenbrot L, Ben-Levy R, et al. Neural expression and chromosomal mapping of Neu differentiation factor to 8p12-p21. Proc Natl Acad Sci USA. 1993;90:1867-1871.

18. Shepard HM, Lewis GD, Sarup JC, et al. Monoclonal antibody therapy of human cancer: taking the HER2 protoncogene to the clinic. J Clin Immunol. 1991;11:117-127.

19. Peles E, Bacus SS, Koski RA, et al. Isolation of the neuHER-2 stimulatory ligand: a 44 kd glycoprotein that induces differentiation of mammary tumor cells. Cell. 1992;69:205-216.

20. Folkman J, Klagsbrun M. Angiogenic factors. Science. 1987;235:442.

21. Ariad S, Seymour L, Bezwoda WR. Platelet-derived

growth factor (PDGF) in plasma of breast cancer patients: correlation with stage and rate of progression. Breast Cancer Res Treat. 1991;20:11-17.

22. Nelson J, Cremin M, Murphy RF. Synthesis of somatostatin by breast cancer cells and their inhibition by exogenous somatostatin and andostatin. Br J Cancer. 1989;59:739-742.

23. Woltering EA, Barrie R, O'Dorisio TM, et al. Somatostatin analogues inhibit angiogenesis in the chick chorioallantoic membrane. J Surg Res. 1991;50:245-251.

24. Zugmaier G, Paik S, Wilding G, et al. Transforming growth factor-beta 1 induces cachexia and systemic fibrosis without an antitumor effect in nude mice. Cancer Res. 1991;51:3590-3594.

25. Koff A, Giordano A, Desai D, Yamashita K, et al. Formation and activation of a cyclin E-cdk2 complex during the G1 phase of the human cell cycle. Science. 1992;257:1689-1694.

26. Miki Y, Swensen J, Shattuch-Eidens D, et al. A strong candidate for the breast and ovarian cancer susceptibility gene BRCA1. Science. 1994;266:66-71.

27. Wooster R, Neuhausen S, Mangion J, et al. Localization of a breast cancer susceptibility gene, BRCA2 to chromosome 13q 12-13. Science. 1994;265:2088-2090.

28. Hall JM, Lee MK, Newman B, et al. Linkage of early onset breast cancer to chromosome 18q21. Science. 1990;250:1684-1689.

29. Shattuck-Eidens D, McClure M, Simard J, et al. A collaborative survey of 80 mutations in the BRCA1 breast and ovarian cancer susceptibility gene. JAMA. 1995;273:535-541.

30. Easton DF, Narod SA, Ford D. The genetic epidemiology of BRCA1. Breast Cancer Linkage Consortium (letter). Lancet. 1994;344:761.

31. Stratton MR, Ford D, Neuhausen S, et al. Familial male breast cancer is not linked to BRCA1 locus on chromosome 17q. Nat Genet. 1994;7:103-107.

32. Rookus MA, vanLeeuwen FE, for the Netherlands Oral

Contraceptives and Breast Cancer Study Group. Oral contraceptives and risk of breast cancer in women aged 20-54 years. Lancet. 1994;344:844-851.

33. Thomas DB. Oral contraceptives and breast cancer: a review of the epidemiologic literature. Contraception. 1991;43:597-642.

34. Romieu I, Berlin JA, Colditz GA. Oral contraceptives and breast cancer: review and meta-analysis. Cancer. 1990;66:2253-2263.

35. Delgado-Rodriguez M, Sillero-Arenas M, Rodriguez-Contreras R, et al. Oral contraceptives and breast cancer: a meta-analysis. Rev Epidemiol Sante Publ. 1991;39:165-181.

36. Jordan A. Toxicology of depot medroxyprogesterone acetate. Contraception. 1994;49:189-201.

37. Paul C, Skegg DCG, Spears GFS. Depot medroxyprogesterone (Depo-Provera) and risk of breast cancer. B Med J. 1989;299:759-762.

38. World Health Organization Collaborative Study of Neoplasia and Steroid Contraceptives. Breast cancer and depot-medroxyprogesterone acetate: a multinational study. Lancet. 1991;338:833-838.

39. Skegg DCG, Noonan EA, Paul C, et al. Depot medroxyprogesterone acetate and breast cancer: a pooled analysis of the WHO and New Zealand Studies. JAMA. 1995;273:799-804.

40. Cobleigh MA, Berris RF, Bush T, et al. Estrogen replacement in breast cancer survivors: a time for change. Breast Cancer Committees of the Eastern Cooperative Oncology Group. JAMA. 1994;272:540-545. (Erratum, JAMA 1995;273:378.)

40a. Colditz BA, Hankinson SE, Hunter DJ, et al. The use of estrogens and progestins and the risk of breast cancer in postmenopausal women. N Engl J Med. 1995;332:1589-1593.

41. Cohen LA, Dendall ME, Zang E, et al. Modulation of N-nitrosomethylurea-induced mammary tumor promotion by dietary fiber and fat. J Natl Cancer Inst. 1991;83:496-501.

42. Willet WC, Stamfer MJ, Coldtiz GA, et al. Dietary fat and the risk of breast cancer. N Engl J Med. 1987;316:22-28.
43. Stampfer MJ, Willett WC, Coldtiz GA, et al. A prospective study of postmenopausal estrogen therapy and coronary heart disease. N Engl J Med. 1985;313:1044-1049.
44. Goldin BR, Aldercreutz H, Gorbach SL, et al. Estrogen excretion patterns and plasma levels in vegetarian and omnivorous women. N Engl J Med. 1982;307:1542-1547.
45. Willet WC, Stampfer, MJ, Coldtiz GA, et al. Relation of meat, fat and fiber intake to the risk of colon cancer in a prospective study among women. N Engl J Med. 1985;323:1664-1672.
46. For review, see Wolfrom D, Welsch CW. Caffeine and the development of normal, benign and carcinomatous human breast tissues: a relationship? J Med. 1990;21:225-250.
47. Adami HO, Sparen P, Bergstrom R, et al. Increasing survival trend after cancer diagnosis in Sweden 1960-1984. J Natl Cancer Inst. 1989;81:1640-1647.
48. Adami HO, Holmberg L, Persson I. Female sex hormones and cancer survival. Lancet. 1994;344:760-761.
49. Bergkvist L, Adami HO, Persson I, et al. Prognosis after breast cancer diagnosed in women exposed to estrogen and estrogen-progesterone replacement therapy. Am J Epidemiol. 1989;130:221-228.
50. Cobleigh MA, et al. Estrogen replacement in breast cancer survivors: a time for change. Breast Cancer Committees of the Eastern Cooperative Oncology Group. JAMA. 1994;272:540-545. (Erratum, JAMA 1995;273:378.)

Chapter 4

Headache

Headache is the most common pain syndrome seen by the physician,[1] and it is estimated that 42 million Americans seek care for the diagnosis and treatment of headache each year.[2] There are several kinds of headaches, each with a different pathophysiology and a different epidemiology. For relief of pain, however, treatment may be much the same, although there are a few important exceptions to this principle.

What Causes Pain in Headaches?

The view that pain in headache is a consequence of vasodilation is largely discredited now; it is much more likely a result of the stimulation of perivascular nociceptive fibers by an unknown mechanism. Precipitating factors include foods, preservatives in foods, stress and a change in sleeping patterns.[3] It is not surprising, then, that the mechanism of pain in migraine is no longer believed to be due to vasodilation. While vasodilation and plasma extravasation do accompany the headache, they are believed to be the consequence of a neurogenic inflammatory response mediated through serotonergic mechanisms. The stimulus causing a headache activates perivascular trigeminal axons; how this happens is still unknown. These axons release vasoactive neuropeptides and promote neurogenic inflammation via antidromic conduction. Simultaneously, via orthodromic conduction along the trigeminal nerves, nociceptive information is carried back to the brain where pain registers.

Alcohol or other vasodilator drugs (like nitroglycerine) that cause headache probably do so not through vasodilation per se, but by stimulating perivascular nociceptive fibers directly. In fact, some drugs used for headache actually promote vasodilation (like calcium channel blockers). Another point against vasodilation as the cause of pain headache is that some migraineurs do not have vasodilation.

Serotonin plays a critically important role in the genesis of headaches. Indeed, the serotonergic system in headache patients may be different from that of normal people,[4] and chronic, possibly inherited, abnormalities in serotonergic pathways may explain the positive family history of headaches in 45-65% of patients.[5,6]

Alterations in serotonin levels accompany headaches; platelet serotonin levels are reduced during pain in both migraine and tension headaches.[7,8] Also, 5-hydroxyindole acetic acid, a serotonin metabolite, is increased.[9]

As estrogen levels increase, serotonin levels also rise.[10] In women, during low-estrogen states such as at menses or during the placebo week of oral contraceptives or estrogen replacement therapy, serotonin levels decrease and headache occurs. During high-estrogen states like pregnancy, serotonin rises and headaches tend to decrease.

Headaches occur less frequently as patients age, and they are aborted by sleep. Both involve the cessation of serotonergic pathways; these stop firing during sleep.[11] There is a decrease in number and size of serotonin-containing neurons at the dorsal raphe (postsynaptic 5-HT_2 receptors) in older patients; this reduction in postsynaptic receptors may be the reason headaches decrease as patients age.[12]

Lowered serotonin levels are also associated with lowered beta endorphin levels, which also helps to increase pain.[13]

Migraine

Migraine headache has an increased prevalence in women (15-17%) compared with men (3-6%).[14] There is no difference until about age 13 in the incidence between girls and boys. As soon as puberty occurs, however, females predominate.[15] Migraines increase in incidence until about 40 years of age and begin to decline thereafter in both sexes. The gender ratio also increases from menarche to about age 42; after that, the difference in incidence between the sexes is less marked. Migraine is defined by Valquist and Bille as a paroxysmal headache characterized by one or more of the following: nausea, scotomata, unilateral pain and a positive family history involving one or more siblings.[16a,16b] Classic migraine headache is unilateral and throbbing. It may be presaged by a warning, or aura, which takes a variety of forms. Scotomata, splitting of the visual field or transient sensory symptoms may all signal a migraine.

Several things seem to precipitate migraine headaches. They tend to occur **after** a particularly stressful period, once the problem or tension has resolved.[17] This may account for their propensity to occur on weekends or during vacations. Others have attributed this latter characteristic to oversleeping, which has produced either hypoglycemia or elevated levels of CO_2.[18] Fasting or missing a meal may also trigger an attack, and others believe migraine could be triggered by chocolate, alcohol and cheeses. Direct acting vasodilators like alcohol, nitrates (abundant in cured meats) and MSG can cause migraine, as can indirect-acting vasodilators like ice cream, caffeine, nicotine, hypoglycemia and MAO inhibitors.

There is an association between migraine and depression; this is another reason some experts have given to explain the prevalence of migraine in women.[19] This is perhaps the reason migraine has been successfully treated with tricyclic antidepressants.[20] These medications are known to work through their influence on serotonin and norepinephrine synthesis and metabolism.

Cluster Headache

In contrast to migraine, cluster headaches are more common in men (7.5:1 and 4:1, depending on series).[21] The age of onset is later than migraine, starting at about 27 to 30 years of age.[22] Like peptic ulcer, which also predominates in men, the peak incidence is seasonal. Experts stress the "somatic virility" of affected males and the "masculine" appearance of the women who suffer the disorder.[23] The mechanism of sex hormone causing or predisposing to the malady, however, may represent more a supersensitivity to testosterone rather than high levels of hormone; in fact, cluster headaches are associated with decreased levels of circulating testosterone.[24] This finding has not been confirmed in other studies.[25] A more complex endocrine matrix is suggested by others, who believe that there is, in fact, an increased sensitivity (upregulation of receptors) to testosterone due to a diminished response to luteinizing hormone (LH), possibly a result of excess epidermal growth factor, which is known to impair gonadal response to LH. This excess of epidermal growth hormone is postulated to be the mechanism of the "leonine facies" that sufferers of cluster headache exhibit.[26]

Daily Headache

The International Headache Society developed and published a new classification of headaches in 1988.[27] Unfortunately, the classification did not include all types of headache, particularly those that are chronic, or that occur almost daily. While they have some features of migraine headaches, they are too frequent to classify as such.[28] Some of these disorders are termed "transformed migraine"; migraine headaches that evolve over years into a daily or near-daily problem with exacerbation during menstrual periods. These patients have more triggers, gastrointestinal symptoms and positive family histories than others; some, but not all, clearly have analgesia-overuse induced headache. Virtually all sufferers are women.[29] These authors have suggested an organizing classification for chronic daily headache. They include the classification of "transformed migraine," in which patients, typically women, have episodic migraine headaches usually beginning in their teens or early adulthood. The associated symptoms of migraine (photophobia, phonophobia and nausea) become less prominent as the headaches become chronic. Indeed, in some patients, classic migraine headaches disappear completely.[30]

Importantly, many chronic headache patients may actually suffer from analgesia-overuse headache. The medications patients use to ward off or to treat headache may themselves produce daily headache.[31] Such patients need detoxification; treatment includes stopping all medication and enduring the period of intensified headaches and, finally, in most patients, improvement occurs.[32]

Headaches in the Athlete

Many authors have described exertionally induced headache, usually labelling them by the nature of the precipitating problem (cough headache, swimmer's migraine, or weightlifter's cephalgia). Mechanisms vary; none are predominant in women.[33]

Sexual Headaches

This peculiar malady, which predominates 3:1 to 4:1 in men, is the occurrence of headache in connection with orgasm. It predominates in the third through the sixth decade of life and may be of several types.[34] The most long lasting is probably due to a meningeal tear during intercourse with subsequent loss of CSF fluid.[35] Beta-blockers are effective in treating sexual headache; it is thought that they work by eliminating or moderating the heart rate related hypertension associated with orgasm.[36] Akpunonu and Ahrens reported successfully treating sexual headache with calcium channel blockers.[34]

Treatment of Headache Pain

Sumatriptan and ergot alkaloids are thought to abort the pain of migraine, cluster headache and even the headache of drug withdrawal through serotonin- receptor-mediated blockade of neurogenic inflammation via pre-junctional mechanisms. Interestingly, since sumatriptan cannot penetrate the blood-brain barrier very well, the receptor site is postulated to be within the meninges.

The treatment of the pregnant or lactating/nursing migraineuse deserves special mention. Migraine worsens during pregnancy in 75% of sufferers.[37] The classic teratogenic period for the human fetus extends from the 31st day to the 10th week after the last menstrual period.[38] In general, the physician must turn from the usual therapeutic interventions and use only acetaminophen or codeine. In the worst cases, IV hydration, narcotics and ice packs may be used. Prednisone can also be tried; it does not cross the placenta as easily as dexamethasone. Silberstein advises lactating women to avoid bromocriptine, ergotamine and lithium and to use benzodiazepam, antidepressants and neuroleptics cautiously.

Some relief is experienced for cluster headaches when patients are treated with testosterone[39] or cyporterone, an antiandrogen that acts like progesterone.[40] The decrease in testosterone production may also be responsible for depression of the cell-mediated immune system: there are more immune disorders in cluster headache patients.[41] The circadian rhythm of testosterone secretion is altered in patients with cluster headaches, with a phase delay of 2 hours.[42] Other investigators have demonstrated a disturbance in the circadian rhythm of melatonin secretion.[43]

The interesting combination of autonomic dysfunction and severe pain in cluster headaches has involved several investigators in work on Substance P, a substance secreted by afferent nerves that are electrically or thermally stimulated, and other tachykinins. They postulate that these entities are released from the sensory trigeminal nerve of the eye and produce pain as well as "vegetative" effects: pupillary constriction, increased thickened saliva, lacrimation and rhinorrhea. Sicuteri and colleagues introduced a novel treatment for cluster headache: capsaicin (a homovanillic acid derivative that is the main noxious component of hot peppers.)[44] This stimulus, placed intranasally, stimulates the nerve trunk and causes accumulation of peptides which block transmission of pain to the cerebral cortex. Other drugs that are useful in treating cluster headache are lithium[45] and calcium entry blockers.[46] Steroids have also been used with some success.[47] Intranasal topical lidocaine and parenteral DHE-45 may also be effective, as is a dose of 100% inhaled oxygen at 6 liters/minute.[48] The amelioration of inflammation is also probably the mechanism for the usefulness of indocin (the treatment of choice for icepick headache) and prednisone (effective in treating cluster headaches).

New products for relief of headache should be aimed at developing substances that selectively activate prejunctional trigeminovascular inhibitory receptors. Hopefully, fewer side effects will also characterize new agents; ergotamines, for example, are contraindicated in pregnancy and in patients with vascular disease. Indeed, virtually all medications now prescribed for the treatment of migraine, cluster or icepick headache have potentially severe side effects.

People who overuse analgesics have a milder, daily headache particularly on awakening, which is described as cap-like, or like a band around the head. Anyone who takes pain medications more than 2-3 days a week for 6-8 weeks or more is at risk for such headaches.[49] The mechanism is possibly downregulation of an already unbalanced serotonergic pain system; aspirin acts to increase the available pool of tryptophan, which is a serotonin precursor. This increases the amount of serotonin, but eventually downregulates the serotonin receptor. Of great interest is the fact that other patients such as arthritics who are not susceptible to headache do not get them from chronic analgesic use.[50] This implies that those who do suffer headaches are particularly susceptible to downregulation of serotonin receptors.

References

1. Solomon GD. Concomitant medical disease and headache. Med Clin North Am. 1991;75:631-639.
2. Mullally WJ. Headache in winter sports. Benign exertional headache. In: Casey MJ, Foster C, Hixson E, eds. Winter Sports Medicine. Philadelphia: FA Davis; 1990:167-175.
3. Moskowitz MA, Macfarlane R. Neurogenic versus vascular mechanisms of sumatriptan and ergot alkaloids in migraine. Trends Pharmacol Sci. 1992;13:307-311.
4. Raskin NH. Headache. 2nd ed. New York: Churchill Livingstone; 1988:109.
5. Bakal DA, Kaganov JA. Muscle contraction and migraine headache; psychophysiologic comparison. Headache. 1977;17:208-215.
6. Ziegler DK, Hassanein R, Hassanein K. Headache syndromes suggested by factor analysis of symptom variables in a headache prone population. J Chron Dis. 1972;25:353-363.
7. Anthony M, Hinterberger H, Lance JW. Plasma serotonin in migraine and stress. Arch Neurol. 1967;16:544-552.
8. Rolf LH, Wiele G, Brune GG. 5-hydroxytryptamine in platelets of patients with muscle contraction headache. Headache. 1981;21:10-11.
9. Curran DA, Hinterberger H, Lance JW. Total plasma

serotonin, 5 hydroxyindoleacetic acid and p hydroxy m methoxymandelic acid excretion in normal and migrainous subjects. Brain. 1965;88:997-1010.

10. Guicheney P, Leger D, Barrat J, et al. Platelet serotonin content and plasma tryptophan in peri- and post-menopausal women: variations with plasma oestrogen levels and depressive symptoms. Eur J Clin Invest. 1988;18:297-304.

11. Aghajanian GK. The modulatory role of serotonin at multiple receptors in the brain. In: Jacobs BL, Gelperin A, eds. Serotonin Neurotransmission and Behavior. Cambridge: MIT Press; 1981:156-185.

12. Wong DF, Wanger HN, Dannals RF, et al. Effects of age on dopamine and serotonin receptors measured by positron tomograph in the living human brain. Science. 1984;226:1393-1396.

13. Leone M. Sacerdote P, D'Amico D, Panerae AE, Bussone G. Beta-endorphin concentrations in the peripheral blood mononuclear cells of migraine and tension-type headache patients. Cephalalgia. 1992;12:155-157.

14. Steward WF, Schecker A, Rasmussen BK. Migraine prevalence: a review of population-based studies. Neurology. 1994;44:817-823.

15. Bille B. Migraine in school children. Acta Paediatr Scand. 1962;51:1-151.

16a. Vahlquist B. Migraine in children. Appl Immunol. 1955;71:348-355.

16b. Bille B. Migraine in school children. Acta Paediatr Scand. 1962;51:1-151.

17. Diamond S. Migraine headaches. Med Clin North Am. 1991;75:545-566.

18. Meyer JS, Dalessio DJ. Toxic vascular headache. In: Dalessio DJ, ed. Wolff's Headache and other Head Pain. 5th ed. New York: Oxford University Press; 1987:136-171.

19. Diamond S. Depression and headache. Headache. 1983;23:122-126.

20. Diamond S. The psychiatric aspects of headache. In:

Cochrane AL, ed. Background to Migraine. New York: Springer-Verlag; 1970:60-64.

21. Manzoni GC, Terzano MG, Bono G, Micieli G, Martucci N, Nappi G. Cluster headache: clinical findings in 180 patients. Cephalalgia. 1983;3:21-30.

22. Ekbom K. A clinical comparison of cluster headache and migraine. Acta Neurol Scand. 1970;46:1-44.

23. Graham JR, Rogado AZ, Rahman M, Gramer IV. Some physical, physiological and psychosocial characteristics of patients with cluster headache. In: Cochrane AL, ed. Background to Migraine. London: W Heinemann; 1970:38-51.

24. Sjaastad O, Salvesen R, Antonaci F. Headache research strategy. Cephalalgia. 1987;7:1-16.

25. Nelson RF. Testosterone levels in cluster and noncluster migrainous headache patients. Headache. 1978;18:265-267.

26. Graham JR. Some clinical and theoretical aspects of cluster headache. In: Saxena PR, ed. Migraine and Related Headache. Rotterdam: Erasmus University; 1975:27-40.

27. Headache Classification Committee of the International Headache Society. Classification and diagnostic criteria for headache disorders, cranial neuralgias and facial pain. Cephalalgia. 1988;8:1-96.

28. Solomon S, Kipton RB, Newman LC. Evaluation of chronic daily headache: comparison to criteria for chronic tension-type headache. Cephalalgia. 1992;12:365-368.

29. For review, see Silberstein SD, Lipton RB, Solomon S, Mathew NT. Classification of daily and near-daily headaches: proposed revisions to the IHS criteria. Headache. 1994;34:1-7.

30. Sandrini G, Manzoni GC, Zanferrari C, Nappi G. An epidemiological approach to the nosography of chronic daily headache. Cephalalgia. 1993;13:72-77.

31. Mathew NT, Kurman R, Perez F. Drug induced refractory headache: clinical features and management. Headache. 1990;30:634-638.

32. Silberstine DS, Appropriate use of abortive medication in headache treatment. Pain Management. 1991;114-121.
33. For review, see Dimeff RF. Headaches in the athlete. Clin Sports Med. 1992;11:339-349.
34. Akpunonu BE, Ahrens J. Sexual headaches: case report, review and treatment with calcium blocker. Headache. 1991;31:131-145.
35. Paulson GW, Klawans HL. Benign orgasmic cephalalgia. Headache. 1974;13:181-187.
36. Littler WA, Honow AJ, Sleight P. Direct arterial pressure, heart rate and electrocardiogram during human coitus. J Reprod Fert. 1974;40:321-331.
37. Uknis A. Silberstein SD. Review article. Migraine and pregnancy. Headache. 1991;31:372-374.
38. Silberstein SD. Headaches and women: treatment of the pregnant and lactating migraineur. Headache. 1993;33:533-540.
39. Klimek A. Use of testosterone in the treatment of cluster headache. Eur Neurol. 1985;24:53-56.
40. Sicuteri F, Poggionin M, Nicolodi M. Marabine S. In: Genazzani AR, Nappi G, Facchinetti F, Martignoni E, eds. Pain and Reproduction. Park Ridge, NJ: Parthenon; 1989:155-161.
41. Giacovazzo M, Martelletti P, Valeri M, Casciani CU. Antigenic characterization in cluster headache and cell mediated immune response to prednisone treatment. In: Sicuteri F, Vecchiet L, Fanciullaci M, eds. Trends in Cluster Headache. Amsterdam: Excerpta Medica; 1987:323-332.
42. Fachinetti F, Nappi G, Cicoli C, et al. Reduced testosterone levels in cluster headache: a stress related phenomenon? Cephalalgia. 1986;6:29-34.
43. Waldenlind E, Ekbom K, Friberg Y, Saaf J, Wettenberg L. Decreased nocturnal serum melatonin levels during active cluster headache episodes. Opusc Med. 1984;29:109-112.
44. Sicuteri F, Fanciullacci M, Nicolodi M, Geppetti P, Fusco BM, Marbine S, Alessandri M, Campagnolo V.

Substance P theory: a unique focus on the painful and painless phenomena of cluster headache. Headache. 1990;30:69-79.

45. Ekborn, K. Lithium for cluster headache: review of the literature and preliminary results of long-term treatment. Headache. 1981;12:132-139.

46. Mullally WJ, Livingston IR, The treatment of chronic cluster headache with nifedipine. Headache. 1984;24:164-165.

47. Kudrow, L. Diagnosis and treatment of cluster headache. Med Clin North Am. 1991;75:579-594.

48. Bracker MD, Rothrock IF. Cluster headaches among athletes. The Physician and Sports-Medicine. 1989;17:137-158.

49. Marcus DA. Serotonin and its role in headache pathogenesis and treatment. Clin J Pain. 1993;2:159-167.

50. Lance F, Parker C, Wilkinson M. Does analgesic abuse cause headaches de novo? Headache. 1988;28:61-62.

Chapter 5

The Heart and Circulation

The female heart is about two-thirds the size of the male heart and has smaller coronary arteries.[1] The differences are not only anatomical; there are important gender-specific differences in normal physiology. At puberty, women's QT interval of the electrocardiogram becomes relatively longer for the same rates than that of males and electrocardiographers must consult tables of normal values in both sexes to correctly interpret tracings.[2]

Women, the QT Interval, and Susceptibility to Sudden Death

Women with the long QT syndrome have an increased incidence of sudden death compared with men who suffer the same disorder. They develop torsades de pointes, a polymorphic ventricular tachycardia that occurs in patients with the long QT syndrome.

Women are also more likely to sustain sudden death during antiarrhythmic therapy than are men, probably because of a basic difference in the biology of membrane channels.[3] In Makkar's search of the literature from 1980-

1992, women comprised 70% of the reported cases of drug-related torsades des pointes. Every drug used (amiodarone, bepridil hydrochloride, disopyramine, proncainamide hydrochloride, prenylamine, quinidine and sotalol hydrochloride) caused torsade in significantly more women than in men—independent of any of the clinical problems described, including electrolyte imbalance. The smaller size of women was not thought to be the reason for their susceptibility: the occurrence of torsade is not related to serum levels of the drugs used. Moreover, there was a greater proportion of women than men with a normal QT in the patients who developed torsade. The authors conclude: "We must consider the possibility that intrinsic cardiac electrophysiologic differences between women and men may explain our observations." The SWORD trial of d-sotalol (Survival With Oral d-Sotalol) which was aimed at testing the effect of sotalol in preventing postinfarction arrhythmia, was discontinued in November,1995[4] because the mortality in treated patients (3.9%) was twice that of placebo (2.0%). Even more relevant from our standpoint was the fact that women had a higher mortality than the males in the group.

Women, Palpitations, and Arrhythmias

After the onset of menarche, "normal" women complain of palpitations more frequently than do men. In a recent report, Romhilt and colleagues monitored the cardiac rhythm of 200 "normal" women between the ages of 20 and 60; they reported that over a quarter of the subjects had premature supraventricular ectopy, and 6% had runs of supraventricular contractions. Over a third had premature ventricular beats; the incidence increased to 48% if women were taking medications including oral contraceptives and thyroid hormone.[5] Of interest is the fact that mean 24 hour heart rate was higher than that reported in young men.[6] Another study reported the results of Holter monitoring of healthy females in their twenties, and found higher rates of atrial premature beats (64%) and ventricular premature beats (54%).[7] Like Romhilt's, this study confirmed the more rapid average heart rates in women as compared with those of men, both during sleep (66 bpm vs. 56 bpm in men) and while awake (90 bpm vs. 80 in men). The more rapid heart rates in women were not due to the fact that men were more exercise-conditioned, as trained athletes were excluded from the study. Given the report of Jose and Collison which established that when beta-blocked and atropinized, both sexes had the same heart rate, it is likely that women have a different autonomic input into their sinus node. Anxiety could not have played a part, since the faster rates in women persisted even during sleep. Brodsky's observations in young males, on the other hand, showed a 56% incidence of atrial premature beats and a 50% incidence of ventricular premature beats.

In comparing these three Holter monitoring studies, two of which looked at females and males in their twenties, it is important to note that the incidence of ectopy was no different between men and women. The only significant difference was in more rapid heart rates in young females and the more frequent marked sinus arrhythmia, bradycardia and incidence of longer sinus pauses in young men. The study in women, however, did not relate the incidence of ectopy to the phase of the menstrual cycle or serum estradiol levels. In the single study that looked at older women (aged 20-59), the incidence of atrial ectopy was 28% compared with much higher rates in the young women (64%) and young men (56%) reported by Rosen's group. The same phenomenon was true of ventricular ectopy(VE): without medication, the rate of VE was 28% in Romhilt's study, while Rosen's group reported a similar incidence (54% in young women vs. 50% in young men) in the two sexes.[6] The reason for the apparent decrease in ectopy as women age was not apparent; it may be due to a higher resting adrenergic tone in younger women versus older women.

Cardiovascular Disease in Women

Cardiovascular disease in women is a significant and largely unappreciated health problem. More women

(478,000) than men (453,000) die each year of cardiovascular disease, and women have almost as many hospitalizations (2.5 million) annually as do men (2.7 million).

Hypertension in Women

More women (9.6 million) than men (8.0 million) have heart disease, and almost as many women (30 million) as men (32 million) have hypertension.[8]

The implications of hypertension in men and women are different, although for both, it is the most important risk factor for stroke.[9] Among men in the Framingham study, the ratio of myocardial infarction (MI) to stroke decreased from 6:1 to 2:1 as blood pressure rose. Among women with similar levels of hypertension, the ratio of MI to stroke was 1:1.2.[10] A dose-response relationship between the number of cigarettes smoked and the risk for stroke is apparent in both men and women, but it is slightly greater for women than for men.[11] While retrospective studies indicate that aspirin use is associated with less frequent myocardial infarction in women, it is not associated with any such effect on stroke.[12] For secondary prevention, though, aspirin is equally effective in men and women; the European Stroke Prevention Study shows that aspirin and dipyridamole are useful in both sexes in reducing the possibility of a second stroke or transient ischemic attack (TIA) after the first ischemic event.[13] The same is true of the prophylactic use of aspirin in atrial fibrillation to prevent an embolic episode: it is equally effective in men and women.[14]

A new study conducted by the National Institute of Neurological Disorders and Stroke investigating the effect of carotid endarterectomy in vessels with at least a 60% obstruction was halted recently because the results of intervention were so powerful. In men, endarterectomy lowered risk by 69%, while in women, although the risk was lower after endarterectomy, it did not reach the level of statistical significance. The reason for the less impressive results in women is unclear.[15]

Peripheral Vascular Disease in Women

The incidence of peripheral vascular disease in women that is severe enough to require surgical intervention is a third that of men.[16] Smoking is the most important risk factor in women for peripheral vascular disease whether they are pre- or postmenopausal; it supersedes, therefore, hormonal protective factors. Mesenteric arterial lesions are much more prevalent in women than in men, while aortic aneurysms are five times more common in men than in women.[17]

This last fact is of particular interest in view of the fact that there is one variant of aorto-iliac disease that seems to be almost exclusively found in middle-aged women: focal, fibrous plaques involving the infrarenal segment of the aorta which are rarely encountered in men.[18] The impact of menopause is about a third as great on the incidence of peripheral vascular disease as it is on coronary artery disease (CAD) in women.[19] The opposite is true of diabetes; diabetic women had a 158% greater incidence of CAD, a 265% greater incidence of ischemic stroke, and a 546% greater incidence of intermittent claudication than nondiabetic women and all the increments were twice the order of magnitude of those in diabetic men.[20]

The impact of surgical (mechanical) intervention seems less effective in women because they tend to have more recurrent stenosis caused by myointimal hyperplasia. This is interesting in view of the fact that women are less likely to have restenosis after coronary angioplasty than are men.[21]

Coronary Artery Disease in Women

Epidemiology

The way coronary artery disease (CAD) is expressed in men and women is significantly different. Since it does not become a major issue for women until later in life (as opposed to men, who face a major risk for CAD by age 45), the lay public and physicians alike largely ignore CAD as a threat to women's lives. Amazingly enough, however, cardiovascular disease kills half a million American women annually. Half of these die of CAD, 20% more than those who die of all cancers combined. In 1989, the National Center for Health Statistics showed that the combined deaths in women from CAD and stroke increased to 98.6/100,000 population, a rate that was more than double all deaths from maternal mortality and breast and gynecological cancer combined (48.6/100,000).[22]

Risk Factors for Coronary Artery Disease in Men and Women

Once a woman is menopausal, her risk for a coronary event quadruples compared with that of women of the same age who are not yet menopausal.[23] The Framingham study, which has now followed a population-based sample of over 5,000 men and women for over 36 years, showed that while the same risk factors pertained to both sexes, they had very different importance depending on the patient's gender. For example, diabetes is twice as important as a risk factor for CAD in women as it is for men, and diabetic women have a greater risk of developing congestive heart failure than do diabetic men. This is explained at least partially by the fact that diabetes in women produces a more atherogenic lipid profile than it does in men.[24]

Interestingly, although experts advise control of risk factors to lessen vulnerability, the National Institutes of Health pointed out recently that trials measuring the impact of doing so on lowering the incidence of coronary artery disease have largely been carried out in men.[25] For example, the National Heart, Lung, and Blood Institute's expert panel could not make a firm recommendation about the advisability of lipid-lowering therapy in women and the elderly as a preventive of CAD because of insufficient data in those categories of patients.[26] John La Rosa, on the other hand, points out that an unpublished meta-analysis of three secondary prevention trials[27] showed that lowering cholesterol in women produced an identical decline in CAD as it did in men. Furthermore, he added, there is a single study in women in which the impact of lowering cholesterol on the regression of coronary artery lesions in patients with familial hypercholesterolemia was studied; women had better results than did the men.[28]

The same questions that should be raised about treatment of hypercholesterolemia in women should be asked about whether or not treating hypertension in women is a useful intervention for preventing CAD; Middeke and colleagues could not find any data to show that treating women with high blood pressure with beta-blockers or diuretics would lower their risk for CAD.[29] The FDA has now instructed its expert reviewers to remind sponsors of clinical trials early in the evaluation process of a new drug that appropriate numbers of women must be included in the study group.[30]

There are interesting differences in risk of dyslipidemia for CAD between the sexes. At menarche, girls' HDL-C levels remain the same, while that of boys falls at puberty.[31] American women's HDL-C levels remain higher than those of men and are a more potent protector against CAD than is the case for American men.[32] The study reported by Davis and associates, though, indicates that there may be crucially important differences in female populations; there was no protective effect of HDL cholesterol in Russian women compared with US women, in whom HDL levels were inversely related to mortality from CAD.[33]

Triglyceride levels are a better predictor of risk in women (especially after the age of 50) than they are for men.[34] This may be more related to the fact that as women age and pass menopause, they manufacture more of the smaller, more dense particles of LDL cholesterol,[35] but this remains to be proved. Diet is less effective in correcting dyslipidemia in women than it is in men,[36] and indeed, dieting in postmenopausal women reduces HDL levels more than it does in men.[37] The same kind of effect is apparent in the consequences of exercise: in men, exercise raises HDL-C and lowers LDL-C more than is the case for women.[38] Central obesity correlates with higher LDL-C and lower HDL-C levels in both sexes, and central obesity is a risk factor for CAD in both.[39]

The normal hormonal fluctuations in women during the phases of the menstrual cycle and during pregnancy have an important impact on serum lipoprotein concentrations. LDL levels decline in the first half of the menstrual cycle and remain low throughout.[40] The changes in pregnancy are complex and, in general, are atherogenic; LDL-C levels increase and remain high well after parturition.[41]

Menopause ushers in further important and negative changes in women's serum lipids: LDL-C levels rise and there is a small decline in individual HDL-C levels.[42]

Oral contraceptives, even newer preparations with lower doses of estrogen, raise LDL-C and lower HDL-C.[43]

Smoking raised the risk for CAD many-fold for women taking older, high-estrogen dose oral contraceptives,[44] but the issue has not been examined adequately in smokers who have been on the newer preparations. Some data suggest that in women under age 35, the synergism between smoking and newer, low dose oral contraceptives seems to be minimal, while smokers age 35 and older have a significantly increased risk of death from circulatory disease.[45]

In meta-analyses of ERT in postmenopausal women, its use has been associated with a much lower incidence of CAD and, indeed, with lower all-cause mortality rates than in women who do not use postmenopausal hormonal replacement therapy.[46] ERT also improved flow-mediated endothelium-dependent vasodilatation in postmenopausal women.[47]

Nabulsi and colleagues have recently showed that the addition of progesterone to estrogen regimens does not lessen and, indeed, may actually improve the favorable impact of HRT on the prevention of CAD.[48]

Clinical Presentation and Course of CAD in Women

The pathophysiology of coronary artery disease in women differs from that in men. Angina pectoris was originally thought to be the first manifestation of the disease in most women (69% of the women followed in the Framingham study presented first with chest pain).[49] It was not until the first report of data from the CASS study which reported the results of cardiac catheterization of men and women with presenting complaints of chest pain[50,51] that it was appreciated that most chest pain in women was not, in fact, angina pectoris, but chest discomfort of noncardiac origin.

Men present more frequently than women (50% vs. 34%) with an acute infarction as the first manifestation of CAD.[52] However, once women have their first myocardial infarction, they have a much higher mortality than do men; in the Framingham cohort, 44% of women died within a year of their first infarction, compared with 27% of men. Women have a higher risk than men of ventricular rupture and early reinfarction.[53,54]

References

1. Killip T. Medical treatment of coronary artery disease in women. In: Wenger NK, Speroff L, Packard B, eds. Cardiovascular Health and Disease in Women. Greenwich: LeJacq Communications Inc; 1993:104-108.
2. Ferrer MI. Electrocardiographic Notebook. 3rd ed. Heober Medical Division. New York: Harper and Row; 1968.
3. Makkar RR, Fromm BS, Steinman RT, Meissner MD, Lehmann HM. Female gender as a risk factor for torsades de pointes associated with cardiovascular drugs. JAMA. 1993;270:2590-2597.
4. Choo V. SWORD slashed. Lancet. 1994;344:1356.

5. Romhilt DW, Chaffin C, Choi SC, Clairborne I. Arrhythmias on ambulatory electrocardiographic monitoring in women without apparent heart disease. Am J Cardiol. 1984;54:582-586.

6. Brodsky M, Wu D, Denes P, Kanakis C, Rosen KM. Arrhythmias documented by 24 hour continuous electrocardiographic monitoring in male medical students without apparent heart disease. Am J Cardiol. 1977;39:390-395.

7. Jose AD, Collison D. The normal range and determinants of the intrinsic heart rate in man. Cardiovas Res. 1970;4:160.

8. Higgins M, Thom T. Cardiovascular disease in women as a public health problem. In: Wenger NK, Speroff L, Packard B, eds. Cardiovascular Health and Disease in women. Greenwich: LeJacq Communications Inc; 1993:15-19.

9. Hershey LA. Stroke prevention in women. Am J Med. 1991;90:288-292.

10. Wolf PA, Kannell WB, Verter J. Current status and risk factors for stroke. Neurol Clin. 1983;1:317-343.

11. Shinton R, Beevers G. Meta-analysis of relation between cigarette smoking and stroke. Br Med J. 1989; 298:789-794.

12. Manson JE, Stamfer MJ, Golditz GA, et al. A prospective study of aspirin use and primary prevention of cardiovascular disease in women. JAMA. 1991;226:521-527.

13. Sivenius J, Riekkinen PJ, Smits P, et al. The European Stroke Prevention Study: results by arterial distribution. Ann Neurol. 1991;29:596-600.

14. Alberts GW, Sherman DG, Gress DR, et al. Stroke prevention in nonvalvular atrial fibrillation: a review of prospective randomized trials. Ann Neurol. 1991;30:511-518.

15. Reported in Internal Medicine. 1994;9(19):1,26.

16. DeBakey ME, Lawrie GM, Glaeser DH. Patterns of atherosclerosis and their surgical significance. Ann Surg. 1985;201:115-131.

17. Hertzer NR. Peripheral vascular disease. In: Wenger NK, Speroff L, Packard B, eds. Cardiovascular Health and Disease in Women. Greenwich: LeJacq Communications Inc; 1993:321.

18. Cronenwett JL, Davis JT Jr, Gooch JB, et al. Aortoiliac occlusive disease in women. Surgery. 1980;88:775-783.

19. Kannel WB, Skinner JJ, Schwartz MJ, et al. Intermittent claudication: incidence in the Framingham Study. Circulation. 1970;41:875-883.

20. Kannell WB, McGee DL. Diabetes and cardiovascular disease: the Framingham study. JAMA. 1979;241:2035-2038.

21. Kelsey SF, James M, Hulubkov AL, et al. (Investigators from the National Heart Lung and Blood Institute Percutaneous Transluminal Coronary Angioplasty Registry.) Results of percutaneous transluminal coronary angioplasty in women. 1985-1986 National Heart, Lung and Blood Institute's coronary angioplasty registry. Circulation. 1993;87:720-727.

22. Wenger NK. Coronary heart disease in women: a "new" problem. Hosp Pract. 1992;27:59-74.

23. Kannell WB, Wilson PWF. Risk factors that attenuate the female coronary disease advantage. Arch Intern Med. 1995;155:57-61.

24. Knopp RH, Broyles FE, Bonet B, Walden CE. Exaggerated lipoprotein abnormalities in diabetic women as compared with diabetic men: possible significance for atherosclerosis. In: Wenger NK, Speroff L, Packard B, eds. Cardiovascular Health and Disease in Women. Greenwich: LeJacq Communications Inc; 1993:133.

25. Palca J. NIH unveils plans for women's health project. Science. 1991;354:792.

26. National Cholesterol Education Program. Report of the expert panel on detection, evaluation and treatment of high blood cholesterol in adults. National Institutes of Health. NIH Publ No 89-2925. Rockville, MD; 1989.

27. Rossouw JR. International trials. Presented at Cholesterol and Heart Disease in Older Persons and in

Women, June 18-19, 1990. National Heart Lung and Blood Institute, NIH, Bethesda, MD.

28. Kane JP, Malloy MJ, Ports TA, et al. Regression of coronary atherosclerosis during treatment of familial hypercholesterolemia with combined drug regimens. JAMA. 1990;264:3007-3012.

29. Middeke M, Holzgreve H. Review of major intervention studies in hypertension and hyperlipidemia: focus on coronary heart disease. Am Heart J. 1988;16:1708-1712.

30. Food and Drug Administration. Statement: women in clinical trials. Dept Health Human Serv, Public Health Serv, FDA, Rockville, MD: October 19, 1992.

31. Rifkind BM, Segal P. Lipid Research Clinics reference values for hyperlipidemia and hypolipidemia. JAMA. 1983;250:1869-1872.

32. Grodon DJ, Probstfield JL, Garrison RJ, et al. High-density lipoprotein cholesterol and cardiovascular disease: four prospective studies. Circulation. 1989;79:8-15.

33. Davis CE, Deev AD, Shestov DB, Perova NV, Plavinskaya SI, Abolafia JM, Kim H, Tyroler HA. Correlates of mortality in Russian and US Women: The Lipid Research Clinics Program. Am J Epidemiol. 1994;139:369-379.

34. Castelli WP. The triglyceride issue: a view from Framingham. Am Heart J. 1986;112:432-437.

35. Campos H, McNamara JR, Wilson PWF, et al. Differences in low density lipoprotein subfractions and apolipoproteins in premenopausal and post-menopausal women. J Clin Endocrinol Metab. 1988;67:30-35.

36. Ernst N, Bowen P, Fisher M, et al. Changes in plasma lipids and lipoproteins after a modified fat diet. Lancet 1980;1:111-113.

37. Barnard RJ. Effects of life-style modifications on serum lipids. Arch Intern Med. 1991;151:1389-1394.

38. Blair SN, Kohn HW II, Paffenbarger RS Jr, et al. Physical fitness and all-cause mortality: a prospective

study of healthy men and women. JAMA. 1989;262:2395-2401.

39. Soler JT, Folsom AR, Kushi LH, et al. Association of body fat distribution with plasma lipids, lipoproteins, apolipoproteins AI and B in postmenopausal women. J Clin Epidemiol. 1988;41:1075-1081.

40. Kim HD, Kalkhoff RK. Changes in lipoprotein composition during the menstrual cycle. Metabolism. 1979;28:663-668.

41. Desoye G, Schweditsch MO, Pfeiffer KP, et al. Correlations of hormones with lipid and lipoprotein levels during normal pregnancy and postpartum. J Clin Endocrinol Metab. 1987;64:704-712.

42. Matthews KA, Meilahn E, Kuller LH, et al. Menopause and risk factors for coronary heart disease. N Engl J Med. 1989;321:641-646.

43. Notelovitz M, Feldman EB, Gillespy M, et al. Lipid and lipoprotein changes in women taking low-dose, triphasic oral contraceptives: a controlled, comparative 12 month clinical trial. Am J Obstet Gyneol. 1989;160:1269-1280.

44. Willet WC, Green A, Stampfer MF, et al. Relative and absolute excess risks of CHD among women who smoke cigarettes. N Engl J Med. 1987;317:1303-1309.

45. Speroff L. The Impact of oral contraception and hormone replacement therapy on cardiovascular disease. In: Wenger NK, Speroff L, Packard B, eds. Cardiovascular Health and Disease in Women. Le Jacq Communications, Inc. 1993:37.

46. Knopp RH. The effects of postmenopausal estrogen therapy on the incidence of arteriosclerotic vascular disease. Obstet Gynecol. 1988;72(suppl 5):23S-30S.

47. Lieberman EH, Gerhard MD, Uehata A, Walsh BW, Selwyn AP, Ganz P, Yeung AC, Creager MA. Estrogen improves endothelium-dependent flow-mediated vasodilation in postmenopausal women. Ann Intern Med. 1994;121:936-941.

48. Nabulsi AA, Folsom AR, Whie A, Patsch W, Heiss G, Wu KK, Szklo M (for the Atherosclerosis Risk in

Communities Study Investigators). Association of hormone-replacement therapy with various cardiovascular risk factors in postmenopausal women. N Engl J Med. 1993;328:1069-1075.

49. Kannel WB, Dawber TR, Kagan A, et al. Factors of risk in the development of coronary heart disease: 6 year follow-up experience. The Framingham Study. Ann Intern Med. 1961;55:33-50.

50. Chaitman BR, Bourassa MG, Davis K, et al. Angiographic prevalence of high-risk coronary artery disease in patient subsets (CASS). Circulation. 1981;64:360-367.

51. Kennedy JW, Killip T, Fisher LD, et al. The clinical spectrum of coronary artery disease and its surgical and medical management: 1974-1979. The Coronary Artery Surgery Study. Circulation. 1982;66 (suppl III) 16-23.

52. Kannel WB, Abbott RD. Incidence and prognosis of unrecognized myocardial infarction: an update on the Framingham Study. N Engl J Med. 1984;311:1144-1148.

53. Marmor A, Sobel BE, Roberts R. Factors presaging early recurrent myocardial infarction ("extension"). Am J Cardiol. 1981;48:603-610.

54. Maeim F, DeLa Maza LM, Robbins SL. Cardiac rupture during myocardial infarction. Circulation. 1972;45:1231-1239.

Chapter 6

Drug Metabolism

Drug dosage and duration of drug effect often depend on the gender of the subject receiving it. Some of the sexual dimorphism is the consequence of differences in hepatic metabolism.

Some differences in drug metabolism in humans that are documented in the literature follow:

Diazepam[1] is cleared more slowly in females until after menopause, when the difference between the sexes disappears.

Paracetamol[2] metabolism is much higher in males because they convert more quickly to the glucuronide; oral contraceptive use increases the rate in females above males.

Clofibrate[3] has a higher rate of glucuronidation in males than females. However, as is the case with paracetamol, oral contraceptives accelerate the rate of glucuronidation in females above that of males.

Isorbide dinitrate[4] is cleared more rapidly in the male than in the female due to degradation to isosorbide mononitrate in the erythrocyte.

Aspirin[5,6] is an example of both sex- and race-related differences in metabolism. In Nigerians, males secreted more free salicylic acid and glucuronide and less glycine conjugated salicyluric acid than women. Overall excretion of free and conjugated salicylic acid was also higher in the male. These data were not true for the Caucasian population.

Skett cautions that gender-specific prescription may in fact be essential to avoid metabolism-related toxicity of the drug.[7]

Hormonal Regulation of Drug Metabolism: Important Features

Androgens

Androgenic control of drug metabolism operates at two levels: first, through the effect of androgen on the brain during development and, second, by maintaining the adult pattern of certain enzymatic activities important to drug metabolism, probably via an effect on the pituitary. There is no known direct effect of androgens on the liver itself. The data for this have been compiled almost exclusively from animal studies. Castration of neonatal male rats, for example, prompts the development of a completely feminine pattern of some essential enzyme activities, i.e., hexobarbitone oxidation in the absence of enzymes usually seen in the male such as 15-beta hydroxylase.[8]

Androgenic effects on the metabolism of many substrates have been demonstrated by: ethylmorphine,[9] aniline,[10] hexobarbitone[18] and p-nitroanisole.[11] The primary site for hepatic drug and steroid metabolism is the hypothalamo-pituitary axis. Growth hormone is the critical substance involved in this regulation. Its pattern of secretion (rather than absolute amounts secreted) is different in the male and female.[12] The levels stay relatively constant in the female, while in the male, there are several peaks of production at 3-4 hour intervals with virtually no detectable hormone in between.[13] The role of somoatostatin, the inhibitor of growth hormone, in regulating hepatic drug metabolism is also apparently crucial.[14] Lesions in the brain that produce a deficiency of somatostatin secretion or the administration of antibodies to somatostatin will produce "feminization" of drug metabolism, (decreasing 6 beta and 16 alpha hydroxylation in hepatic microsomes). In the male, somatostatin secretion will blunt the peak secretion of growth hormone and inhibit the male pattern of hepatic metabolism. Somatostatin secretion pattern in the male is probably set during development by androgenic imprinting of the developing brain; neonatal castration of the male rat produced a feminine pattern of growth hormone secretion.[15]

Skett cautions that the pituitary control of drug metabolism probably involves other elements besides growth hormone. He points out that inadequate growth hormone secretion during the neonatal period has a less marked effect on hepatic drug metabolism than if it were the sole controlling factor.

Pancreatic Hormones and Control of Hepatic Metabolism of Drugs

In rats, spontaneous or experimentally induced diabetes can affect hepatic drug metabolism, indicating that pancreatic hormones exert significant control of the cytochrome P-450 system. For example, Skett and Joels demonstrated that diabetes mellitus inhibited male-specific metabolism of diazepam, lignocaine and imipramine.[16] There are also modifying effects of diabetes on some, but not all, aspects of female-specific drug metabolism; i.e., an increase in 7-alpha hydroxylation was heightened by diabetes mellitus but there was no effect on 5-alpha reductase in female rats.[17,18] Insulin reversed all the effects of diabetes on hepatic drug metabolism. Skett, reviewing the available data on this phenomenon, proposed that insulin and testosterone have a final common pathway in controlling hepatic drug metabolism, i.e., their impact on growth hormone. Diabetes causes a marked change in growth hormone secretory pattern.[19] It is of interest, though, that this effect on growth hormone secretion persists long after the effect on drug metabolism, suggesting that growth hormone is not the only controlling influence on liver function in drug processing. Work in tissue culture suggests that growth hormone is a "feminizing" element and insulin a "masculinizing" substance on drug metabolism.[20]

Cytochrome P-450 System in Males and Females

There is a sex-specific difference in the activity of the cytochrome P-450 system in the rat,[21] mouse[22] and trout.[23] Convincing corroborating data include high-performance liquid chromatography (HPLC) separation of solubilized microsomal preparations that are different between the sexes.[24] Other data have shown that the P-450 II and III families are male-specific.[25] The presence of these sexually dimorphic isoenzymes is under the control of growth hormone, gonadal hormones and the hypothalamus. Less well-studied, but also implicated in sex-specific differences in drug metabolism is NADPH cytochrome P-450 reductase. Replacement of the male-derived reductase with female-derived enzyme causes a significant lowering in the concentration of lignocaine N-deethylase, a male-specific enzyme. Lignocaine 3-hydroxylase, on the other hand, which is not sexually dimorphic, shows no change in concentration.[26]

There are age-related changes in the P-450 enzyme systems that may feminize drug metabolism; the male rat liver demonstrates senescent-associated changes that produce feminization of drug-metabolizing ability.[27] Hooper and Sui Qing's study on the pharmacokinetics of mephobarbital supports the notion that the same is true of humans; mephobarbital was metabolized more actively in a group of young men (aged 18-25) than in young or older women, or in older men.[28]

The lipid layer in which the cytochrome system is embedded is also sexually dimorphic. Male-specific enzymes are inhibited if they are isolated and re-embedded in female derived lipids.[29] Moreover, once embedded in this lipid environment, at least one male-specific enzyme (lignocaine N-deethylase) demonstrated a female-specific pattern, showing the important influence of the lipid bilayer on the sexual dimorphism of the P-450 system. Indeed, important changes in lipid composition occur in pregnancy and correlate with alterations in drug metabolism during gestation.[30,31]

Mechanism of Hormonal Control of Drug Metabolism

There are solid data to suggest that hormones act on both of the second messenger systems to impact on P-450 activity. One is the cyclic adenosine monophosphate (c-AMP) system. C-AMP activates protein kinase and causes phosphorylation of acceptor proteins. C-AMP itself can phosphorylate cytochrome P-450 to produce the degraded form (cytochrome P-420); reconstitution of the degraded system produces reduced enzymatic activity.[32,33]

The other second messenger system involved in the regulation of drug metabolism is phosphatidylinositol (PI) turnover. Increasing PI breakdown increases intracellular free calcium and activates protein kinase C. glucagon, which inhibits hepatic drug metabolism[34] and impacts both the c-AMP and PI systems. Thus, the impact of some hormones on second messenger systems may be complex.

Interactions Between Drugs and Oral Contraceptives

In an informative review, Back and Orme summarized the interactions between oral contraceptives and other drugs.[35] Interactions can be of two types. Some drugs can impair the efficacy of oral contraceptive steroids (e.g., many of the anticonvulsant drugs, with the exception of valproic acid). The molecular basis of such an interaction is the induction of specific forms of cytochrome P-450 (P-

4590 IIC and IIIA) which accelerates the clearance of the oral contraceptives. Two drugs, ascorbic acid (vitamin C) and paracetamol (acetaminophen) increase the concentration of ethinylestradiol; they compete with the latter for sulphation. Oral contraceptives reduce the clearance of a number of medications that undergo oxidation; among them diazepam, alprazolam, nitrazepam, theophylline, prednisolone, caffeine and cyclosporin. In contrast, they increase clearance of drugs that undergo glucuronidation (salicylic acid, temazepam, acetaminophen, morphine and clofibric acid).

Gender Differences in the Pharmacology of Psychotropic Medication

Although most studies for optimal dosages of psychotropically active substances have been done in males, women seek and receive more of this medication than do men.[36]

There are very little direct experimental data available to explain observed differences in the serum levels and length of action of some drugs in male and female subjects despite weight and age matching, but there are several examples of such differences. Yonkers and colleagues summarized the most important data in their recent review[37] and offered the following general statements: (1) Women in general have higher plasma levels of psychotropic drugs especially if they are on oral contraceptives; and (2) Antipsychotic agents not only have greater effectiveness in women, but women are more likely to suffer adverse reactions such as hypothyroidism and dyskinesia.

The concern about many of the pharmacological sex differences has stimulated a conference sponsored by the National Women's Health Resource Center in Washington, D.C.; a published report is now available.[38]

References

1. MacLeod SM, Giles HG, Bengert B, Liu FF, Sellers EM. Age and gender related differences in diazepam pharmacokinetics. 1979. J Clin Pharmacol. 1979;19:15-19.
2. Miners JO, Attwood J, Birkett DJ. Influence of sex and oral contraceptive steroids on paracetamol metabolism. Brit J Clin Pharmacol. 1983;15:503-509.
3. Miners JO, Robson RA, Birkett DJ. Gender and oral contraceptive steroids as determinants of drug glucuronidation: effects on clofibric acid elimination. Brit J Clin Pharmacol. 1983;18:240-243.
4. Bennett BM, Twiddy DAS, Moffat JA, Armstrong PW, Marks GS. Sex-related differences in the metabolism of isosorbide dinitrate following incubation in human blood. Biochem Pharmacol. 1983;32:3729-3734.
5. Emudianughe TS, Oduleye SO, Ebadab EE, Eneji SD. Sex differences in salicylic acid metabolism in Nigerian subjects. Xenobiotica. 1986;16:177-179.
6. Caldwell J, O'Gorman J, Smith RL. Interindividual differences in the glycine conjugation of salicylic acid (proceedings). Brit J Clin Pharmacol. 1980;9(70):114.
7. Skett P. Biochemical basis of sex differences in drug metabolism. Pharmac Ther. 1988;38:269-304.
8. Yates FE, Herbst AL, Urquhart J. Sex differences in the rate of ring A reduction of delta-4-3-ketosteroids in vitro by rat liver. Endocrinology. 1958;63:887-902.
9. el-Masry S el D, Mannering GJ. Sex dependent differences in drug metabolism in the rat: II. qualitative changes produced by castration and the administration of steroid hormones and phenobarbital. Drug Metab. Dispos. 1974;2:279-284.
10. Quinn GP, Axelrod J, Brodie BB. Species, strain and sex differences in metabolism of hexobarbitone, amidopyrine, antipyrine and aniline. Biochem Pharmacol. 1958;1:152-159.
11. Bell JH, Ecobichon DJ. The development of kinetic parameters of hepatic drug metabolizing enzymes in perinatal rats. Can J Biochem. 1974;53:433-437.

12. Yamozoe Y, Shimada M, Murayama N, Kawano S, Kato R. Effects of hypophysectomy and growth hormone treatment on sex-specific forms of cytochrome P-450 in relation to drug and steroid metabolisms in rat liver microsomes. Jap J Pharmacol. 1986;42:371-382.

13. Eden S. Age and sex-related differences in episodic growth hormone secretion in the rat. Endocrinology. 1979;105:555-560.

14. Norstedt G, Mode A, Hokfelt T, Eneroth P, Elde R, Ferland L, Labrie F, Gustafsson JA. Possible role of somatostatin in the regulation of the sexually differentiated steroid metabolism and prolactin receptor in rat liver. Endocrinology. 1983;112:1076-1090.

15. Jansson JO, Ekberg S, Isaksson O, Mode A, Gustafsson JA. Imprinting of growth hormone secretion, body growth and hepatic steroid metabolism by neonatal testosterone. Endocrinology. 1985;117:1881-1889.

16. Skett P, Joels LA. Different effects of acute and chronic diabetes mellitus on hepatic drug metabolism in the rat. Biochem Pharmacol. 1985;34:287-289.

17. Skett P. Sex dependent effects of streptozotocin-induced diabetes mellitus on hepatic steroid metabolism in the rat. Acta Endocrinol. 1986;111:217-221.

18. Warren BL, Pak R, Finlayson M, Gontovnick L, Sunahara G, Bellward GD. Differential effects of diabetes on microsomal metabolism of various substrates; comparison of streptozotocin and spontaneous diabetic Wistar rats. Biochem Pharmacol. 1983;32:327-335.

19. Tannenbaum GS. Growth hormone secretory dynamics in streptozotocin diabetes: evidence for role of endogenous circulating somatostatin. Endocrinology. 1981;108:72-82.

20. Hussin AH, Skett P. The effect of insulin on steroid metabolism in isolated rat hepatocytes. Biochem Pharmacol. 1987;36:3155-3159.

21. Kato R, Kamataki T. Cytochrome P-450 as a determinant of sex differences of drug metabolism in the rat. Xenobiotica. 1982;12:787-800.

22. Harada N, Negishi M. Mouse liver testosterone 15

alpha hydroxylase (cytochrome P-450): purification, regioselectivity, stereospecificity and sex-dependent expression. J Biol Chem. 1984;259:1256-1271.

23. Williams DE, Masters BSS, Lech JJ, Buhler DR. Sex differences in cytochrome P-450 isozyme composition and activity in kidney microsomes of mature rainbow trout. Biochem Pharmacol. 1986;35:2017-2023.

24. Fujita S, Kitagawa H, Chiba M, Suzuki T, Ohta M, Kitani K. Age and sex associated differences in the relative abundance of multiple species of cytochrome P-450 in rat liver microsomes: a separation by HPLC of hepatic microsomal cytochrome P-450 species. Biochem Pharmacol. 1985;34:1861-1864.

25. Waxman DJ. Interactions of hepatic cytochromes P-450 with steroid hormones: regioselectivity and stereospecificity of steroid metabolism and hormonal regulation of rat P-450 enzyme expression. Biochem Pharmacol. 1988;37:71-84.

26. Barr J. Sex differences in drug and steroid metabolism in rat liver: biochemical basis. University of Glasgow. Thesis. 1985.

27. Fujita S, Chiba M, Ohta M, Kitani K, Suzuki T. Alteration of plasma sex hormone levels associated with old age and its effect of hepatic drug metabolism in rats. J Pharmacol Exp Ther. 1990;253:369-374.

28. Hooper WD, Sui Qing M. The influence of age and gender on the stereoselective metabolism and pharmacokinetics of mephobarbital in humans. Clin Pharmacol Ther. 1990:48:633-640.

29. Barr J, Skett P. The role of cytochrome P-450, NADPH-cytochrome P-450 reductase and lipids in sex differences in hepatic drug metabolism. Brit J Pharmacol. 1984;83:396.

30. Turcan RG, Tamburini PP, Gibson GG, Parke DV, Symons AM. Drug metabolism, cytochrome P-450 spin state and phospholipid changes during pregnancy in the rat. Biochem Pharmacol. 1981;30:1223-1226.

31. Belina H, Cooper SD, Farkas R, Feuer G. Sex differences in the phospholipid composition in rat liver

microsomes. Biochem Pharmacol. 1975;24:301-303.
32. Taniguchi H, Pyerin W, Stier A. Conversion of hepatic microsomal cytochrome P-450 to P-420 upon phosphorylation by cyclic AMP dependent protein kinase. Biochem Pharmacol. 1985;34:1835-1837.
33. Pyerin W, Taniguchi H, Horn F, Oesch F, Amelizad A, Freidberg T, Wolf CR. Biochem Biophys Res Comm. 1987;142:885-892.
34. Weiner M, Buterbaugh GG, Blake CA. Inhibition of hepatic drug metabolism dycyclic 3'5' adenosine monophosphate. Res Comm Chem Path Pharmacol. 1972;3:249-263.
35. Back DJ, Orme ML'E. Pharmacokinetic drug interactions with oral contraceptives. Clin Pharmacokinet. 1990;18:472-484.
36. Kessler RC, Brown RL, Broman CL. Sex differences in psychiatric help-seeking: evidence from four large-scale surveys. J Health Soc Behav. 1981;22:49-64.
37. Yonkers KA, Kando JC, Cole JO, Blumenthal S. Gender differences in pharmacokinetics and pharmacodynamics of psychotropic medication. Am J Psychiatry. 1992;149:587-595.
38. Hamilton JA, ed. Clinical pharmacology panel report. In: Blumenthal SJ. Forging a Women's Health Research Agenda. Conference Proceedings. Washington DC: National Women's Health Resource Center. 1991.

Chapter 7

Immunology

Women have higher immunoglobulin levels than men[1] and a higher incidence of immunologically based illnesses. This is consonant with their ability to mount more vigorous immune responses to *E. coli*[2] and the infecting agents of hepatatis B,[3] brucella,[1] measles,[4] and rubella[5] than do men. Their cell-mediated immune response is less vigorous than that of men[6] but, on the other hand, they mount a more vigorous response to viral illnesses and parasitic infestations.[7]

Pregnancy dampens the intensity of the immune response. Cell-mediated immunity is diminished[8] as is natural killer (NK) cell activity.[9] Even in the nonpregnant woman, progesterone seems to promote a lessening of the immune response at times when implantation might occur. It fosters, for example, the production of immunologically active (suppressor) substances by proliferative endometrium but has no such effect on secretory endometrium.[10] NK cell activity is depressed just before ovulation.[11] Hertz has gone so far as to view menstruation as an estrogen-progesterone-mediated cyclic autoimmune process.[12]

The relationship of sex hormones to immunological processes is a close one, and many examples exist of the relationship of gonadal hormones on immune-competent cells. In general, estrogen stimulates humoral and cell-mediated immunity, while testosterone does the opposite. 17-Beta-estradiol receptors exist on CD8-positive T cells,[13] thymic cells,[14] and mononuclear cells.[14] Conversely, there are no known testosterone receptors on the cells in the peripheral blood.[15] Progesterone injected intra-articularly relieves inflammation, probably due to its supression of interleukin-1 production by monocytes.[16] Menopausal women have an increased release of interleukin-1 by monocytes which reverses if they receive hormonal replacement therapy.[17]

Another immunologic function of estrogen is its effect on B cell lymphopoiesis, described by Kincade and colleagues recently.[18] Interleukin-7 is an essential cytokine for B cell lymphopoiesis. The precursors of interleukin-7 are depressed during normal pregnancy as soon as 6 days after conception.[19] The data suggest that the production of new B cells as well as their export from marrow is severely limited during pregnancy. A combination of estrogen in very low doses and progesterone was synergistic in depressing B-lineage precursors. Nursing prolongs this phenomenon, as it does depression of the thymus.[20,21] Gonadal hormones influence immune responses differently. Estradiol and tamoxifen stimulate immunoglobulin synthesis by B cells by inhibiting suppressor T cell activity.[22] Testosterone, in contrast, inhibits or has no effect on the same process.[23]

Given these data, it is not surprising that autoimmune diseases show a distinct preponderance in women. The female-male ratios for many are elevated: systemic lupus erythematosus (SLE), 9:1; Sjogren's syndrome, 10:1; rheumatoid arthritis (RA), 7:1 in premenstrual women decreasing to 3:1 postmenopausally; and multiple sclerosis, 2:1.[24] Predictably the menstrual cycle and pregnancy have an effect on the severity of these diseases. Premenstrual flare-ups of SLE and RA are common[25,26] and, indeed, both RA and SLE have been reported to show abnormalities in the production and/or metabolism of sex hormones.[27-29] Pregnancy ameliorates the symptoms of rheumatoid arthritis,[30] whereas lupus increases in severity during the first trimester, normalizing later in pregnancy.[31]

Oral contraceptives modify the course of rheumatoid

arthritis, particularly if they contain norethynorel and mestranol.[32] Oral contraceptives containing only progesterone or postmenopausal doses of estrogen ameliorate SLE,[33] but high estrogen/progesterone combinations make it worse.[34] There are also data that suggest that oral contraceptives can induce some features of lupus in women who have either false positive serum tests for syphilis or who have had manifestations of rheumatoid arthritis.[33]

The effects of the gonadal steroids seem to be mediated through special receptors which in effect dissociate the androgenic or estrogenic effects from their impact on immunologic function.[35] Schuurs and Verheul suggest that an innovative research path might be to modify gonadal steroids so that they might have desirable immunologic impact, but be free of other hormonal effects.[36] Vamvakopoulos and Chrousos suggest that corticotropin releasing hormone (CRH) may, in fact, be responsible for the sexual dimorphism of the immune/inflammatory reaction and the difference in the prevalence of autoimmune diseases between the sexes.[37] They showed that estrogen stimulated transcriptional regulation of the CRH gene, and believe that the CRH gene was an important target of ovarian steroids. Thus, they postulate that estrogen is the mediator of gender-related differences in the stress response and HPA axis activity. CRH coordinates the stress response and the regulation of the immune/inflammatory reaction.[38] CRH is secreted centrally, where it inhibits the reproductive and growth axes, as well as the immune system, and stimulates the sympathetic nervous system.[39] It is also produced peripherally, where it stimulates inflammatory reactions.[40] Markedly elevated secretion of immune CRH in inflammatory sites has been demonstrated in an animal model of increased susceptibility to autoimmune inflammatory disease.[41]

References

1. Rhodes K, Scott A, Markham RL, Monk-Jones ME. Immunological sex differences. Ann Rheum Dis. 1969;28:104-119.

2. Michaels RH, Rogers KD. A sex difference in immuno-logic responsiveness. Pediatrics. 1971;47:120-123.
3. London WT, Drew JR. Sex differences in response to hepatitis B infection among patients receiving chronic dialysis treatment. Proc Natl Acad Sci USA. 1977;74:2561-2564.
4. Patty DW, Furesz J, Boucher DW. Measles antibodies as related to HLA types in multiple sclerosis. Neurology. 1976;26:651-655.
5. Spencer MJ, Cherry JD, Powell KR, Mickey MR, Terasaki PI, Mary SM, Sumaya CV. Antibody responses following rubella immunisation analysed by HLa and ABO types. Immunogenetics. 1977;4:365-372.
6. Inman RD. Immunologic sex differences and the female preponderance in systemic lupus erythematosus. Arthritis Rheum. 1978;21:480-484.
7. Ansar AS, Penhale WJ, Talal N. Sex hormone, immune responses and autoimmune diseases. Am J Path. 1985;125:531-551.
8. Thong YH, Steele RW, Vincet MM, Hensen SA, Bellanti JA. Impaired in vitro cell-mediated immunity to rubella virus during pregnancy. N Engl J Med. 1973;289:604-606.
9. Gabrilova J, Zadjelovic J, Osmak,M, Suchanek E, Zapnivic A, Boranic M. NK cell activity and estrogen hormone levels during normal human pregnancy. Gynec Obstet Invest. 1988;15:167-172.
10. Wang HS, Kanzaki H, Tokushige M, Sato S, Yoshida M, Takahide M. Effect of ovarian steroids on the secretion of immunosuppressive factors from human endometrium. Am J Obstet Gynecol. 1988;158:629-637.
11. Sulke AN, Jones DB, Wood PJ. Variation in natural killer activity in peripheral blood during the menstrual cycle. Br Med J (Clin Res Ed). 1985;290:884-886.
12. Hertz R. Hypothesis: menstruation is a steroid-regulated, cyclic, autoimmune process. Am J Obstet Gynec. 1986;155:374-375.
13. Cohen JHM, Danel L, Gordier G. Saez S, Revillard JP. Sex steroid receptors in peripheral T cells: absence of

androgen receptors and restriciton of estrogen receptors to OKT 8 positive cells. J Immunol. 1983;131:2767-2771.

14. Danel L, Sovweine G, Monier JC, Saez S. Specific estrogen binding sites in human lymphoid cells and thymic cells. J Steroid Biochem. 1983;18:559-563.

15. Cohen JHM, Danel L, Gordier G, Saez S, Revillard JP. Sex steroid receptors in peripheral T cells: absence of androgen receptors and restriction of estrogen receptors to OKT8 positive cells. J Immunol 1983;131:2767-2771.

16. Cuchacovich M, Tchernitchin A, Gatica H, Wurgaft R, Valenzueal C, Cornejo E. Intraarticular progesterone effects of a local treatment for rheumatoid arthritis. J Rheumatol. 1988;15: 561-565.

17. Pacifici R, Rifas L, McCracken R, Vered I, McMurtry C, Avioli LV, Peck WA. Ovarian steroid treatment blocks a postmenopausal increase in blood monocyte interleukin 1 release. Proc Natl Acad Sci USA. 1989;86:2398-2402.

18. Kincade PW, Medina KL, Smithson G. Sex hormones as negative regulators of lymphopoiesis. Immunol Rev. 1994;137:119-134.

19. Lee G, Namen AE, Gillis S, Ellingsworth LR, Kincade PW. Normal B cell precursors responsive to recombinant mure IL-7 and inhibition of IL-7 activity by transforming growth factor beta. J Immunol. 1989;142:3875-3883.

20. Medina KL, Smithson G, Kincade PW. Suppression of B lymphopoiesis during normal pregnancy. J Exp Med. 1993;178:1507-1515.

21. Ito T, Hoshino T. Studies of the influences of pregnancy and lactation on the thymus in the mouse. Seitschrift fur Zellforschung. 1962;57:667.

22. Paaveone T, Andersson LC, Adlercreutz H. Sex hormone regulation of in vitro immune response: estradiol enhances human B cell maturation via inhibition of suppressor T cells in pokeweed mitogen stimulated cultures. J Expl Med. 1981;154:1935-1945.

23. Sthoeger ZM, Chiorazzi N, Lahita RG. Regulation of the immune response by sex hormones: in vitro effects of estradiol and testosterone on pokeweed mitogen induced human B cell differentiation. J Immunol. 1988;141:91-98.
24. Inman Rd. Immunologic sex differences and the female preponderance in systemic lupus erythematosus. Arthritis Rheum. 1978;21:849-852.
25. Lahita RG. Sex steroids and rheumatic diseases. Arthritis Rheum. 1985;28:126-131.
26. Rudge SR, Kavank JC, Drury PL. Menstrual cyclicity of finger joint size and grip strength in patients with rheumatoid arthritis. Ann Rheum Dis. 1983;42:425-430.
27. Inman RD. Systemic lupus erythematosus in the male: a genetic and endocrine study. Arthritis Rheum. 1979;22:624.
28. Lahita RG, Kunel HG, Bradlow HL. Increased oxidation of testosterone in systemic lupus erythematosus. Arthritis Rheum. 1983;26:1517-1521.
29. Lahita RG, Bradlow HL, Ginzler E, Pang S, New M. Low plasma androgens in women with systemic lupus erythematosus. Arthritis Rheum. 1987;30:241-248.
30. Hench PS. The ameliorating effects of pregnancy on the chronic atrophic (infectious rheumatoid) arthritis, fibrositis and interior heat hydrarthrosis. Mayo Clin Proc. 1938;13:161-168.
31. Friedman EA, Rutherford JW. Pregnancy and lupus erythematosus. Obstet Gynecol. 1956;8:601-610.
32. Gilbert M, Rothstein J, Cunningham C, Estrin I, Davidson A, Pincus G. Norethynodrel with mestranol in treatment of rheumatoid arthritis. J Am Med Assn. 1964;190:147.
33. Jungers P, Dougados M, Pelissier C, Kuttenn P, Tron F, Lesavre P, Bach JF. Influence of oral contraceptive therapy on the activity of systemic lupus erythematosus. Arthritis Rheum. 1982;25:618-623.
34. Pimstone BL. Systemic lupus erythematosus exacerbated by oral contraceptive. S Afr J Obstet Gynecol. 1966;4:62-63.

35. Giguere V, Yang N, Segui P, Evans RM. Identification of a new class of steroid hormone receptors. Nature. 1988;331:91-94.
36. Schuurs HW, Verheul HA. Effects of gender and sex steroids on the immune response. Steroid Biochem. 1990;35:157-172.
37. Vamvakopoulos NC, Chrousos GP. Evidence of direct estrogenic regulation of human corticotropin-releasing hormone gene expression. J Clin Invest. 1993;92:1896-1902.
38. Bateman A, Singh A, Kral T, Solomon S. The immune-hypothalamic-pituitary-adrenal axis. Endocr Rev. 1989;10:92-112.
39. Chrousos GP, Gold PW. The concepts of stress and stress system disorders: overview of physical and behavioral homeostasis. JAMA. 1992;267:1244-1252.
40. Karalis K, Sano H, Redwine J, Listwak S, Wilder RL, Chrousos GP. Autocrine or paracrine inflammatory actions of corticotropin releasing hormone in vivo. Science. 1991;254:421-423.
41. Sternberg EM, Hill HM, Chrousos GP, Kamilaris T, Listwak S, Gold PW, Wilder RL. Inflammatory mediator-induced hypothalamic-pituitary-adrenal axis activation is defective in streptococcal cell wall arthritis-susceptible Lewis rats. Proc Natl Acad Sci. 1989;86:2374-2378.

Chapter 8

Intestinal Function

The Irritable Bowel Syndrome

The irritable bowel syndrome (IBS), present in 11-14% of adults in the western world and China, is the most common disorder of the gastrointestinal tract.[1] In fact, 40-60% of patients seen in gastrointestinal clinics in the Western hemisphere have some form of this disorder.[2] It affects women three times as frequently as men, and whites five times more than blacks. In women, it is one of the causes of chronic pelvic pain, including dyspareunia, which is the result of a tender colon.[3] The disease appears first in late adolescence or early adulthood, but prevalence is greatest between 45 and 64 years of age.[4,5] The cost and effort involved is staggering: more than 2 million medications and 3 million physician visits per year are for the treatment of IBS. [6,7] It is second only to the common cold as the most frequent cause of absence from work.[8]

Many gastroenterologists consider IBS more a disorder of the psyche than of the gut. This attitude, however, is changing as our understanding of gut innervation expands.

91

The notion that there is a structural and biochemical basis for the disorder, rather than its simply existing in the perception of the sufferer, is consonant with the observation that most patients with the syndrome never consult a physician.[9] It may be, however, that social and cultural factors impact on this; women in western cultures seek medical care for IBS symptomatology more frequently than men, but the reverse is true in India.[10] Also of interest is the observation that the placebo response in IBS therapy varies from 40-70%.[11]

The diagnosis of irritable bowel syndrome is notoriously imprecise and it is very likely that a number of subtypes have been lumped together. Indeed, gastroenterologists have not yet agreed on what criteria to use for the diagnosis. The International Congress of Gastroenterology in Rome defined it in 1986 as a constellation of symptoms including: abdominal pain relieved by defecation, an alteration in the frequency or consistency of stool, and/or disturbed defecation.[12] This definition takes into account the apparent contradiction in the fact that IBS sufferers frequently report both constipation and diarrhea. Several investigators using different techniques correlated constipation with delayed transit time, and diarrhea with increased transit time, of liquids and solids in IBS patients.[13-15] Other experts offer different criteria. Manning lists four: the presence of loose stools at the onset of pain, more frequent bowel movements when pain begins, pain relieved by defecation, and abdominal distention.[16] Talley's group adds the presence of mucus per rectum and a sensation of incomplete evacuation, symptoms also listed by Manning, but not believed by him to be discriminatory.[17] Symptoms may vary between the sexes; however, a 1991 study[18] looked at the fit of Manning's four principal and two minor criteria for IBS in patients diagnosed as having IBS simply on the basis of having abdominal pain, altered bowel habits, or both, in the absence of demonstrable gastrointestinal disease. Manning's diagnostic criteria fit female patients quite precisely, but did not do so for men and were not useful for the diagnosis of IBS in the male patient.

Until recently, investigators trying to unravel the pathophysiology of IBS concentrated almost exclusively on the colon. Small intestinal motility, however, is also likely to be disturbed in IBS. Its malfunction, moreover, is closely associated with the pain that characterizes this syndrome.

The innervation of the upper gastrointestinal tract and the small intestine is better understood and defined than that of the colon.[19,20] The mechanical activity of the small intestine (called the migrating motor complex or MMC) has three phases: a period of quiescence is followed by random irregular contractile activity which ends in a brief burst of continuous phasic contractions. The interval between MMCs varies widely between persons and even within individuals. It is importantly influenced by the time of day (patterns are diurnal),[21] region, age,[22] and the menstrual cycle.[23]

Some experts believe that the characteristic pattern of small intestinal motility is disordered in IBS. Thompson and colleagues reported that phase II, the period of random irregular contractions, is prolonged and never culminates in phase III, the coordinated sustained phasic contractions. It is this pattern that accompanies the experience of pain in the sufferer.[24] This finding was confirmed by others.[25] In the normal distal ileum, another distinctive complex, a high-amplitude and very propulsive, rapidly propagated wave exists.[26] Patients with IBS experienced pain in association with this type of contraction significantly more often than did normal subjects.[27]

There is conflicting information about whether or not the response of small intestinal motility to food is different from that of normal people in patients with IBS. Some workers have described an increase in motility accompanied by pain after a meal in patients in whom diarrhea was a prominent symptom of their disease, while constipation-prone individuals with IBS had a blunted response when fed.[28] Others believe that bowel motility is similar postprandially in normal and IBS patients.[29] The confusion is probably due to the difficulty in obtaining artifact-free recordings over a long enough period of time and in the choice of different locations in the small intestine made by various teams of investigators.

The relationship of particular foods to IBS is of interest. Various foods seem to be problematic in specific areas of the world, such as malabsorbed sugars, particularly lactose,[30] and in Danish patients, fructose and sorbitol.[31] Further support for the idea that certain foods are a luminal irritant in susceptible IBS patients appears in the work from England showing a significant and prolonged improvement with systematic dietary exclusions.[32] Finally, there is no question that the ileal mucosa is abnormally sensitive to bile acids in IBS, responding with increased secretion and bile acid malabsorption. This results in the presentation of short or medium chain fatty acids to the right colon; these induce rapidly propagated massive contractions accompanied by diarrhea and/or pain.[33]

Over half the patients with IBS reported exacerbation of their symptoms with stress.[34] In response to stress, IBS patients' contractile patterns changed dramatically and, in some, were abolished altogether.[35] Nevertheless, some studies fail to demonstrate a relationship between stress and IBS.[36] Whitehead studied a group of women with IBS, however, and found that they had significantly more stressful life events (he corrected the data for what he termed the "confounding influence of neuroticism"), but interestingly enough found only a slightly greater degree of correlation between self-reported stress and change in bowel function (about 10% greater than controls); even normal patients reported that psychological stress caused a difference in their bowel symptoms.[37] For men with IBS, stress centered around worries about their careers, while women with the disorder worried most about their families.[38a,38b] These studies are about three decades old; it would be interesting to repeat them now to see whether or not these data are reproducible in the present social climate.

Finally, the association of physical and/or sexual abuse with IBS is significant: 53% of female clinic patients report maltreatment compared with 37% of control patients.[39]

This finding was recently confirmed by a study of women with painful gastrointestinal disorders, including 13 with gastroesophageal reflux disease (GERD), 26 with noncardiac chest pain (NCCP), and 11 with IBS. Again, 56% reported sexual/physical abuse; 82% of patients with IBS answered affirmatively, as did 92% of those with GERD. In contrast, only 27% of patients with NCCP (comparable to controls) reported such mistreatment. Abused patients had significantly lower pain thresholds.[40]

The troublesome symptom of abdominal distention in IBS is probably best related to delayed passage and stagnation of gut contents; Trotman and Price demonstrated delayed ileal emptying and impaired ileocecal clearance in patients with this complaint.[41] Whorwell and his group believe IBS is essentially a global disorder of visceral smooth muscle, offering data that document impaired lower esophageal sphincter tone and esophageal dysmotility in IBS patients.[42] About half of IBS patients describe symptoms of esophageal dysfunction.[43a,43b] Other experts, however, attribute this to altered pain perception rather than to real dysmotility.[44] In fact, some suggest that IBS symptomatology is essentially the consequence of a perceptual disorder, either peripherally or centrally mediated. This abnormal perception of normal events produces a disturbance in the motility of the gastrointestinal tract.[45] In their comprehensive review of the IBS literature, McKee and Quigley conclude that, in fact, there is no good data to support the idea of a essential disturbance in colonic motility in IBS; they suggest, in fact, that food ingestion and stress produce "an exaggerated colonic motor response".[46a] Nevertheless, while IBS patients report pain at a lower threshold of balloon distention than normal subjects (attributed to neuroticism), they also experience rectosigmoid spasm at lower pressures than others and, significantly, are no more sensitive than others to other types of pain. In short, their sensitivity and their response with spasm to lesser degrees of intestinal distention is specific, characteristic and severe.[46b] Whitehead and Crowell make the trenchant observation that when the psychological profiles of lactose-intolerant patients (who have symptoms identical with those of IBS sufferers) are compared with IBS patients there is no difference except in those IBS sufferers who elect to consult a physician. Thus, neurosis or psychological distress is not the etiology of IBS; these factors were more evident only in patients who consulted a physician about symptoms. This was as true of women as of men.[47] Furthermore, a case might be made that a lifetime of suffering from the symptoms of irritable bowel syndrome might well create emotional or psychic distress in any individual, particularly if the symptoms are severe enough to compel the patient to seek medical attention. I have not been able to find any study that compares the severity of symptoms in the IBS patient who seeks medical attention with one who does not—probably for the obvious reason that the latter is not identifiable in the course of patient selection for a clinical trial or epidemiological study.

In a thoughtful recent editorial, Almy attempts to reconcile the two divergent views of the etiology of IBS. He points out that there is no contradiction between the scholarship that emphasizes the role of the central nervous system and that which concentrates on the unique neuromuscular physiology of the gut in trying to explain this disorder. In fact, the enteric nervous system is a remarkably complex and effective organ (which Almy refers to as a "little brain" or "computer") and has an intricate, bidirectional communication with the central nervous system.[48]

The only generally agreed upon therapy for IBS sufferers is loperamide for patients with diarrhea, which decreases small bowel secretion and dampens gut motility; bran or psyllium for constipation[49]; 1-beta galactoside for flatus; and amitriptyline for chronic pain.[50] More recently, in a small series of female patients with IBS, in whom symptoms are known to fluctuate in relationship to their menstrual cycle, leuprolide (a gonadotropin-releasing hormone analogue that downmodulates pituitary gonadotropins and thereby inhibits sex hormone production) significantly improved symptoms. The provocative suggestion that IBS in women is a completely different disease than in men underlies the observations of Smith[32] that Manning's clinical criteria fit women with the syndrome but not men, who seem to be a small subset of patients with a somewhat distinct disorder different from that which women experience.[51]

Cholelithiasis

Women develop gall bladder disease more frequently than do men. Their risk changes with age, illustrating the impact of female hormones on the disorder. Before menopause they are four times more likely to develop gallstones than are men; however, after menopause, they continue to have a twofold higher risk.[52,53]

The composition and lithogenicity of bile varies with the phases of the menstrual cycle, and both pregnancy and the older, high-dose estrogen oral contraceptives increase the tendency of women to form stones.[54] Progesterone decreases gall bladder contractility and may further enhance the tendency of women to develop stones because of stasis.[55]

The lithogenicity of bile is related in part to the ratio of primary to secondary bile acids in the bile[56] which is lower in women than in men. Deoxycholic acid, a secondary acid formed by intracolonic bacterial degradation of cholic acid, when reabsorbed increases not only risk for cholelithiasis but for cancer of the colon. The well-known trophic effects of bile on intestinal mucosa,[57] as well as the erosive action of unconjugated deoxycholic acid[58] on the lining of the gut, may explain the higher incidence of Crohn's disease (50% higher in women than in men) and ulcerative colitis in women. The exacerbation of inflammatory bowel disease in pregnancy[59] and its occurrence in women who begin using oral contraceptives[60] implicate sex hormones in the pathogenesis of the disease.

Bowel Transit Time in Women

Bowel transit time is slower in women than in men,[61] particularly premenopausally[62] which may account for the self-reported three times higher rate of constipation in women than in men.[63] This feature of women's normal physiology might explain the higher incidence of colonic cancers in females compared with that in men. Of interest is the propensity of colonic cancer in women to be grouped toward the proximal rather than the distal colon, another observation that may be explained by the relatively longer transit time deoxycholic acid and perhaps other carcinogenic substances linger in the colon in women.[64] Fecal weight, which reflects the extent of intracolonic bacterial fermentation of dietary fiber and the amount of residual fiber and its associated water content,[65] is greater in men than in women, even in studies that control for diet.[66] This difference is most marked between men and pre-menopausal women.[67] Stool pH in women is more alkaline than that of men.[68] This may be a the result of less complete bacterial fermentation of dietary fiber in females compared with males. Sex hormones actually influence the population of colonic bacteria; intestinal bacteria produce anti-neoplastic substances called lignans.[69a,69b] In women, urinary excretion of lignans is higher in the luteal phase of the menstrual cycle and in early pregnancy.[69a,70]

Idiopathic Slow Transit Constipation

A syndrome of severe constipation found exclusively in young women under 35 was first described in 1909.[71] Preston and Lennard-Jones studied a series of 64 women with intractable symptoms who had an unusual combination of slow total gut transit time and a normal colon width on barium enema.[72] The authors speculate that colonic innervation is disordered in these women; they cannot expel feces without digital pressure on the puborectalis muscle, which does not relax normally during defecation but contracts instead. They also have a blunted appreciation of rectal and bladder distention, hesitancy in starting micturition, syncope and an increased incidence of Raynaud's phenomenon, all of which suggest a generalized disturbance of the autonomic nervous system. A hormonal imbalance may also be an etiologic factor: many patients said their only spontaneous bowel movements occurred during their menstrual period, and the group had a higher incidence than normal of ovarian cysts. Of interest were the failure of these women to respond to laxative or fiber therapy and the fact that they could not be demonstrated to be more psychologically disturbed than other patients with disorders of the intestinal tract.

Pregnancy and The Intestinal Tract

Pregnancy has a special impact on bowel disorders. There are an estimated 5.5 million pregnancies a year in the United States, although about a fifth of these are aborted.[73] Pregnancy has little effect on gut secretion and absorption but significantly changes its motility and tone. The lower esophageal sphincter, for example, relaxes in the gravid patient, with the result that 50-80% of women complain of heartburn, particularly when lying down.[74] An interesting study in transsexual men showed that combination hormonal therapy produced the same relaxation of the sphincter as did pregnancy in women, but estrogen alone did not, implying that the effect was due to progesterone.[75] Estrogen is probably necessary as a "primer" for progesterone to affect the sphincter; estrogen alone produced no effect.[76]

Treatment for peptic ulcer disease or hyperacidity in pregnancy must be restricted to the following medications: antacids, (although they may interfere with iron absorption); sodium bicarbonate (which may cause metabolic alkalosis and fluid overload in both the mother and fetus)[77]; and sucralfate (which is not absorbed and produces almost complete remission of heartburn).[78] Most information about H2 blockers in pregnancy comes from animals: all of these medications cross the placenta and are excreted in breast milk. Cimetidine produces feminization of adult male rats.[79] Omeprazole, at many times the usual human dose, disrupts pregnancies in rabbits and rats.

Nausea and vomiting in pregnancy can be extremely troublesome and it has been suggested that they are probably the consequence of progesterone's inhibiting action of visceral motility.[80] In fact, altered gastric motility has been demonstrated by cutaneous electrodes positioned over the abdomen in all nauseated pregnant women without exception. Motility cycles included tachygastrias, bradygastrias, and in some patients, a flat line pattern.[81]

The literature about nausea and vomiting in pregnancy reflects the sexism of some physicians. In 1943, Menninger went so far as to say these symptoms represented an attempt (albeit unconscious) to reject the unwanted fetus.[82] Unfortunately, the view of the nauseated pregnant woman as psychically disturbed persists and, 40 years after Menninger's remark, another investigator opined that such women are more likely to have negative relationships with their own mothers.[83] Therapy for the nausea and vomiting of pregnancy is based on frequent small feedings that are high in carbohydrates and low in fat content. Antiemetics may be teratogenic.[84] Vitamin B6 relieved some women after 3 days of treatment, and severe (although not mild) nausea was significantly diminished.[85] The salicylates in bismuth subsalicylate may be absorbed. They are teratogenic in animals and may cause hemorrhage in the newborn child.[86]

Abdominal bloating and constipation during pregnancy are common. Small bowel transit time is decreased[87] and correlates with a decrease in plasma motilin, a stimulatory gastrointestinal hormone.[88] Progesterone inhibited colonic motility in animal experiments,[89] but data on the precise mechanics of colon function in pregnant humans are not available. Of relevance, however, is the finding that colonic transit times were the same in men and women, no matter what phase of the menstrual cycle women were in, and even if they were on oral contraceptives.[90] Laxatives during pregnancy are fraught with peril: anthraquinones cause congenital malformation[91] and castor oil may precipitate labor. Saline laxatives like milk of magnesia may overload the fetus and mother with salt, while mineral oil used in excess may prevent absorption of fat-soluble vitamins, with consequent hemorrhaging in the newborn.[92] Bulk forming agents, because they are not absorbed, are the preferred treatment for constipation in the pregnant patient.

There are interesting and age-related differences between men and women in the rates of gastric emptying of liquids and solids.[93] No matter what their age, women had slower gastric emptying of liquids than did men. In contrast, postmenopausal women and men had equal transit times for solids, but premenopausal women and women on hormonal replacement therapy had slower times than men.

In contrast to the basal state, in which gender-specific differences are apparent in gut transit time, exercise increases oral to cecal transit time in both men[94] and women[95] to a comparable extent. The response is probably due at least in part to increased cortisol levels. However, serum titers of motilin and gastrin remain the same as in the resting state.

References

1. Thompson WG. Irritable bowel syndrome: prevalence, prognosis and consequences. Can Med Assoc J. 1986;134:111-113.
2. Lennard-Jones JE. Functional gastrointestinal disorders. N Engl J Med. 1983;308:431-435.
3. Whorwell PJ, McCallum M, Creed FH, Roberts CT. Noncolonic features of irritable bowel syndrome. Gut. 1986;27:37-40.
4. Schuster MM. Diagnostic evaluation of the irritable bowel syndrome. Gastroenterol Clin North Am. 1991;20:269-278.
5. Schuster MM. Irritable bowel syndrome: new perspectives on management. Cleveland Clin J Med. 1993;60:270-271.
6. National Center for Health Statistics. Plan and operation of the second National Health and Nutrition Examination Survey 1976-80: programs and collection

procedures. Series 1, No 15. DHHS Publ No (PHS) 81:1317. Hyattsville, MD. US Dept HHS. July, 1981.

7. Sandler RS. Epidemiology of irritable bowel syndrome in the United States. Gastroenterology. 1990;99:409-415.

8. Almy TP. Digestive disease as a national problem. II. White paper by the American Gastroenterological Association. Gastroenterology. 1967;53:821.

9. Thompson, WG. Irritable bowel syndrome: pathogenesis and management. Lancet. 1993;341:1569-1572.

10. Thompson WG, Creed F, Dossman DA, Heaton KW, Mazzacca G. Functional bowel disorders and functional abdominal pain. Gastroenterol Int. 1992;5:75-91.

11. Thompson WG. Irritable bowel syndrome: pathogenesis and management. Lancet. 1993;341:1569-1572.

12. Thompson WG, Dotevall G, Drossman DA, Heaton KW, Kruis W. Irritable bowel syndrome: guidelines for the diagnosis. Gastroenterol Int. 1989;2:92-95.

13. Cann PA, Read NW, Brown C, Hobson N, Holdsworth CD. Irritable bowel syndrome: relationship of disorders in the transit of a single solid meal to symptom patterns. Gut. 1983;24:405-411.

14. Jian R, Vigneron N, Najean Y, Bernier JJ. Gastric emptying and intragastric distribution of lipids in man: a new scintigraphic method of study. Dig Dis Sci. 1982;27:705-711.

15. Jian R, Majea Y, Bernier JJ. Measurement of intestinal progression of a meal and its residues in normal subjects and patients with functional diarrhea by a dual isotope technique. Gut. 1984;25:728-731.

16. Manning AP, Thompson WG, Heaton KW, Morris AF. Towards positive diagnosis of the irritable bowel. Br Med J. 1978;2:653-654.

17. Talley NJ, Phillips SF, Melton LJ, Mulvihill C, Wiltgen C, Zinsmeister AR. Diagnostic value of the Manning criteria in irritable bowel syndrome. Gut. 1990;31:77-81.

18. Smith RC, Greenbaum DS, Vancouver JB, Henry RC, Reinhart MA, Greenbaum RB, Dean HA, Mayle JE.

Gender differences in Manning criteria in the irritable bowel syndrome. Gastroenterology. 1991;100:591-595.

19. Quigley EM. Small intestinal motor activity: its role in gut homeostasis and disease. Q J Med. 1987;65:799-810.

20. Stancui C, Bennett JR. The general pattern of gastro-duodenal motility 24 hour recordings in normal subjects. Rev Med Chir Soc Med Nat Iasi. 1975;79:31-36.

21. Thompson DG, Wingate DL, Archer L, Benson MJ, Green WJ, Hardy RJ. Normal patterns of upper small bowel motor activity recorded by prolonged radiotelemetry. Gut. 1980;21:500-506.

22. Kellow JE, Brorody TJ, Phillips SF, Tucker RL, Haddad AC. Human interdigestive motility: variations in patterns from esophagus to colon. Gastroenterology. 1986;91:386-395.

23. Wald A, VanThiel DH, Hoechstatter L, Gavaler JS, Egler KM, Verm R, Scott L, Lester R. Gastrointestinal transit: the effect of the menstrual cycle. Gastroenterology. 1981;80:1497-1500.

24. Thompson DG, Laidlow SM, Wingate DL. Abnormal small-bowel motility demonstrated by radiotelemetry in a patient with irritable colon. Lancet. 1979;2:1321-1323.

25. Kellow JE, Gill RC, Wingate DL. Prolonged ambulant recordings of small bowel motility demonstrate abnormalities in the irritable bowel syndrome. Gastroenterology. 1990;98:1208-1218.

26. Quigley EM, Borody TJ, Phillips SF, Wienbeck M, Tucker RL, Haddad A. Motility of the terminal ileum and ileocecal sphincter in healthy humans. Gastroenterology. 1984;87:857-866.

27. McKee DP, Quigley EM. Intestinal motility in irritable bowel syndrome: is IBS a motility disorder Part 2: motility of the small bowel, esophagus, stomach and gall bladder. Dig Dis Sci. 1993;38:1773-1782.

28. Kellow JE, Miller LJ, Phillips SF, Zinsmeister AR. Dysmotility of the small intestine in irritable bowel syndrome. Gut. 1988;29:1236-1243.

29. Thompson DG, Wingate DL, Archer L, Benson MJ, Green WJ, Hardy RJ. Normal patterns of upper small bowel motor activity recorded by prolonged radiotelemetry. Gut. 1980;21:500-506.

30. Bayless TM, Rosensweig NS. A racial difference in incidence of lactase deficiency: a survey of milk intolerance and lactase deficiency in healthy adult males. JAMA. 1966;197:9688-9692.

31. Rumessen JJ, Gudmand-Hoyer E. Functional bowel disease: malabsorption and abdominal distress after ingestion of fructose, sorbitol and fructose-sorbitol mixtures. Gastroenterology. 1988;95:694-700.

32. Nanda R, James R, Smith H, Dudley CR, Jewell DP. Food intolerance and the irritable bowel syndrome. Gut. 1989;30:1099-1104.

33. Camilleri M, Prather CM. The irritable bowel syndrome: mechanisms and a practical approach to management. Ann Int Med. 1992;116:1001-1008.

34. Hislop IG. Psychological significance of the irritable colon syndrome. Gut. 1971;12:451-457.

35. Kumar D, Wingate DL. The irritable bowel syndrome: a paroxysmal motor disorder. Lancet. 1985;2:973-977.

36. Ford MJ, Miller PM, Eastwood J, et al. Life events, psychiatric illness and the irritable bowel syndrome. Gut. 1987;28:160-165.

37. Crowell MD, Whitehead WE, Heller B, et al. Prospective evaluation of stressful life events on bowel symptoms in a large community sample. Gastroenterology. 1990;98:A341.

38a. Chaudhary NA, Truelove SC. The irritable colon syndrome: a study of the clinical features, predisposing causes and prognosis in 130 cases. Q J Med. 1962;31:307-323.

38b. Hill OW, Blendis L. Physical and psychological evaluation of "nonorganic" abdominal pain. Gut. 1967;8:221-229.

39. Drossman DA, Leserman J, Nachman G, et al. Sexual and physical abuse in women with functional or

organic gastrointestinal disorders. Ann Intern Med. 1990;113:828-833.

40. Scarinci IC, McDonald-Haile J, Bradley LA, Richter JE. Altered pain perception and psychosocial features among women with gastrointestinal disorders and history of abuse: a preliminary model. Am J Med. 1994;97:108-118.

41. Trotman IF, Price CC. Bloated irritable bowel syndrome defined by dynamic^{99m}Tc bran scan. Lancet. 1986;2:364-366.

42. Whorwell PJ, Clouter C, Smith CL. Oesophageal motility in the irritable bowel syndrome. Br Med J (Clin Res Ed). 1981;282:1101-1102.

43a. Watson WC, Sullivan N, Corke M, Rush D. Incidence of oesophageal symptoms in patients with irritable bowel syndromes. Gut. 1976;17:827A.

43b. Stark GA, McMahon TP, Richter JE. Increasing evidence for the irritable gut syndrome. Gastroenterology. 1987:92:1652A.

44. Richter JE, Barish CF, Castell DO. Abnormal sensory perception in patients with esophageal chest pain. Gastroenterology. 1986;91:845-851.

45. Mayer EA, Raybould HE. Role of visceral afferent mechanisms in functional bowel disorders. Gastroenterology. 1990;99:1688-1704.

46a. McKee DP, Quigley EMM. Intestinal motility in irritable bowel syndrome: is IBS a motility disorder. Part 1: Definition of IBS and colonic motility. Dig Dis Sci. 1993;38:1761-1772.

46b. Whitehead WE, Holtkotter B, Enck P, et al. Tolerance for rectosigmoid distention in irritable bowel syndrome. Gastroenterology. 1990;98:1187-1192.

47. Whitehead WE, Crowell MD. Psychologic considerations in the irritable bowel syndrome. Gastroenterol Clin North Am. 1991;20:249-267.

48. Almy TP. Management of the irritable bowel syndrome: different views of the same disease. Ann Int Med. 1992;116:1027-1028.

49. Health KW. Role of dietary fibre in irritable bowel syn-

drome. In: Read NW, ed. Irritable Bowel Syndrome. London: Grune & Stratton; 1985:203-222.

50. Thompson WG. Irritable bowel syndrome: pathogenesis and management. Lancet. 1993;341:1569-1572.

51. Mathias JR, Clench MH, Reeves-Darby VG, et al. Effect of leuprolide acetate in patients with moderate to severe functional bowel disease. Dig Dis Sci. 1995;40:1405-1407.

52. Newman HF, Northup JD. Collective review: the autopsy incidence of gallstones. Int Abst Surg. 1959;109:1-13.

53. Lindstrom CG. Frequency of gallstone disease in a well-defined Swedish population: a prospective necropsy study in Malmo. Scan J Gastroenterol. 1977;54:7-10.

54. McMichael AJ, Potter JD. Reproduction, endogenous and exogenous sex hormones and colon cancer: a review and hypothesis. J Natl Cancer Inst. 1980;65:1201-1207.

55. Bennion LJ, Grundy SM. Risk factors for the development of cholelithiasis in man. N Engl J Med. 1978;299:1161-1167.

56. Fisher MM, Yousef IM. Sex differences in the bile acid composition of human bile: studies in patients with and without gallstones. Can Med Assoc J. 1973;109:190-193.

57. Williamson RC. Intestinal adaptation. Part II: mechanisms of control. N Engl J Med. 1978;298:1444-1450.

58. Dietschy JM. Effects of bile salts on intermediate metabolism of the intestinal mucosa. Fed Proc. 1967;26:1589-1598.

59. Mogadam M, Korelitz BI, Ahmed SW. The course of inflammatory bowel disease during pregnancy and postpartum. Am J Gastroenterol. 1981;75:265-269.

60. Husson J. Ileite (maladie de Crohn probable) et oestroprogestatifs. Sem Hop Paris. 1981;57:1750-1751.

61. Gear JSS, Brodribb AJM, Ware A. Fibre and bowel transit times. Br J Nutr. 1981;45:77-82.

62. Brauer PM, Slavin JL, Marlett JA. Apparent digestibili-

ty of neutral detergent fiber in elderly and young adults. Am J Clin Nutr. 1981;34:1061-1070.

63. National Center for Health Statistics. Prevalence of selected chronic digestive conditions: United States, 1975. DHEW publication PHS 79-1558. Vital and health statistics, series 10, no 123. Hyattsville, MD, 1979.

64. McMichael AJ, Potter JD. Do intrinsic sex differences in lower alimentary tract physiology influence the sex-specific risk of bowel cancer and other biliary and intestinal diseases? Am J Epidemiol. 1983;118:620-627.

65. Stephen AM, Cummings JH. Mechanism of action of dietary fibre in the human colon. Nature. 1980;284:283-284.

66. Cummings JH, Stephen AM, Wayman B, et al. Influence of age, sex and dose on colonic response to dietary fibre from bread. Gastroenterology. 1979;76:1116.

67. Brauer PM, Slavin JL, Marlett JA. Apparent digestibility of neutral detergent fiber in elderly and young adults. Am J Clin Nutr. 1981;34:1061-1070.

68. Stephen AM, Cummings JH. The effect of wheat fiber on faecal pH in man . Gastroenterology. 1981;80:1294.

69a. Setchell KDR, Lawson AM, Mitchell F, et al. Lignans in man and in animal species. Nature. 1980;287:740-742.

69b. Axelson M, Setchell KD. The exretion of lignans in rats: evidence for an intestinal bacterial source for this new group of compounds. FEBS Lett. 1981;123:337-342.

70. Setchell KD, Lawson AM, Borriello SP, et al. Lignan formation in man: microbial involvement and possible roles in relation to cancer. Lancet. 1981;2:4-7.

71. Lane WA. Chronic intestinal stasis. Br Med J. 1909;1: 1408-1411.

72. Preston DM, Lennard-Jones JE. Severe chronic constipation of young women: "idiopathic slow transit constipation". Gut. 1986;27:41-48.

73. Monthly Vital Statistics Report. 1992;40:1-20.

74. Bassey OO. Pregnancy heartburn in Nigerians and Caucasians with theories about aetiology based on manometric recordings from the oesophagus and stomach. Br J Obstet Gynaecol. 1977;84:439-443.
75. Filippone M, Malmud L, Kryston L, Antonucci J, Bottger J, Fisher RS. Esophageal and LES pressures (LESP) in male transsexuals treated with female sex hormones. Clin Res. 1983;31:282A. Abstract.
76. Van Thiel DH, Wald A. Evidence refuting a role for increasing abdominal pressure in the pathogenesis of heartburn associated with pregnancy. Am J Obstet Gynecol. 1981;140:420-422.
77. Lewis JH, Weingold AB. The use of gastrointestinal drugs during pregnancy and lactation. Am J Gastroenterol. 1985;80:912-923.
78. Rachet G, Gangemi O, Patron M. Sucralfate in the treatment of gravidic pyrisos. Giornale Italiano de Ostericia Ginecologia. 1990;12:1-16.
79. Parks S, Schade RR, Pohl CR, Gravaler JS, VanThiel DH. Prenatal and neonatal exposure of male rat pups to cimetidine but not ranitidine adversely affects subsequent adult sexual functioning. Gastroenterology. 1984;86:675-680.
80. Kumar D. In vitro inhibitory effect of progesterone on extrauterine human smooth muscle. Obstetrics. 1962;25:729-734.
81. Koch KL, Stern RM, Vasey M, Botti JJ, Creasy GW, Dwyer A. Gastric dysrhythmias and nausea of pregnancy. Dig Dis Sci. 1990;35:961-968.
82. Wemmens JP. Female sexuality and life situations: an etiologic psycho-socio-sexual profile of weight gain and nausea and vomiting in pregnancy. Obstet Gynecol. 1971;38:555-563.
83. Fitzgerald CM. Nausea and vomiting in pregnancy. Br J Med Psychol. 1984;57:159-165.
84. MacMahon B. More on Bendectin. JAMA. 1981;246:371-372.
85. Sahakian V, Rouse D, Sipes S, Rose N, Niebyl J. Vitamin B6 is effective therapy for nausea and vomit-

ing of pregnancy: a randomized, double-blind placebo-controlled study. Obstet Gynecol. 1991;78:33-36.

86. Collins E. Maternal and fetal effects of acetominophen and salicylates in pregnancy. Obstet Gynecol. 1978;58:57-62.

87. Wald A, Van Thiel DH, Hoechstetter L, Gavaler JS, Egler KM, Verm R, et al. Effect of pregnancy on gastrointestinal transit. Dig Dis Sci. 1982;27:1015-1018.

88. Christofides ND, Ghatei MA, Bloon SR, Borberg C, Gillmer MD. Decreased plasma motilin concentrations in pregnancy. Br Med J. 1982;285:1453-1454.

89. Ryan JP, Bhojwani A. Colonic transit in rats: effect of ovariectomy, sex steroid hormones and pregnancy. Am J Physiol. 1986;251:G46-50.

90. Hinds JP, Stoney B, Wald A. Does gender or the menstrual cycle affect colonic transit? Am J Gastroenterol. 1989;84:123-126.

91. Nelson MM, Forfar JO. Association between drugs administered during pregnancy and congenital abnormalities of the fetus. Br Med J. 1971;1:523-527.

92. Berkowitz RL, Cousten DR, Mochizcki TK, eds. Handbook for Prescribing Medications during Pregnancy. Boston: Little, Brown & Co; 1981.

93. Hutson WR, Roehrkasse RL, Wald A. Influence of gender and menopause in gastric emptying and motility. Gastroenterology. 1989;96:11-17.

94. Keeling WF, Martin BJ. Gastrointestinal transit during mild exercise. J Appl Physiol. 1987;63:978-981.

95. Keeling WF, Harris A, Martin BJ. Orocecal transit during mild exercise in women. J Appl Phsyiol. 1990;68:1350-1353.

Chapter 9

Saliva

There are very few specific data on gender and oral hygiene. The most useful literature concerns the causes of caries, gingivitis and bad breath; none present information that is gender specific.

Halitosis

Bacterial putrefaction causes bad breath; bacteria degrade proteins and amino acids.[1] In particular, degradation of sulphur containing amino acids such as cysteine, cystine and methionine are particularly offensive.[2] The mucosal epidermal cells and saliva provide these substrates. Moreover, saliva itself carries oxygen which, paradoxically, although it improves halitosis, also fosters more bacterial fermentation. Thus, saliva itself facilitates oxygen depletion and secondarily contributes to malodor. An acid pH is critical to the process; acidity inhibits malodor production, while pHs above 6.5 promote fermentation.[3] The bacteria that contribute to this adhere to the epithelial cells of the mucosa. The degree of halitosis is directly related to the number of organisms that are gram-negative; these organisms degrade amino acids when oxygen is present and are responsible for about 80% of mouth oxygen consumption.[4] Gram-positive bacteria are most efficient at fermenting carbohydrates in an aerobic environment.[5]

Individuals with higher numbers of bacteroides and fusobacteria degrade salivary protein more rapidly than others.[6,7] Also important is the concentration of proline and glutamate that is present, as these deplete oxygen very rapidly and promote halitosis.

The thickness of plaque, which is related to inaccessibility to oral hygienic measures, irregularity of mucosal surfaces (such as the dorsum of the tongue, where it is thick), and lack of salivary contact, is an important determinant of halitosis. In a thicker plaque, bacteria in inner, unstirred layers are more likely to flourish in an anaerobic environment.[8] Gingival inflammation increases as gram-negative anaerobic bacteria multiply. The end products of their metabolism, which include ammonia, butyrate, hydrogen sulfide and methyl mercaptan, are not only malodorous but also injure periodontal tissues. Saliva has an efficient buffering capacity. Its rapid flow and the consequent repeated washings of plaque help keep pH down.[9,10] The reason for foul morning breath is in part related to low salivary flow rates and a lack of oxygen in the oral cavity.

Salivary flow rates, buffer capacity and yeast counts were tested in 187 patients over the age of 20; men had higher resting and stimulated salivary flow rates than women. Patients with medication had significantly lower flow rates and less buffering capacity than unmedicated subjects, particularly in the over 60 age group. Men had more positive yeast counts than did women, unless the patients were medicated, when the differences became nonsignificant.[11] Occlusal wear is greater in men than in women. The difference is enhanced by age, increased bite force, decreased occlusal tactile sensitivity and the absence of crowding. Low salivary buffer capacity and low flow rates increased occlusal wear.[12]

Saliva should be monitored particularly in selected disease states; depression, for example, is accompanied by decreased salivary flow rates. This may be related in part to diminished food intake and antidepressant medications, but is probably also a primary effect of depression.[13] Diabetics have reduced flow rates; this has been found to be related inversely to levels of glycosylated hemoglobin.[14] If diabetes is well controlled, however, salivary flow rates do not differ from age and sex matched controls.[15] HIV disease affects the salivary gland in about 6% of patients,[16] and some investigators have suggested that research in HIV infected patients might provide useful information about how viruses produce immunologically mediated salivary gland pathology.[17]

There are circadian rhythms in the electrolyte and glucose content of saliva in both sexes.[18] Some vary with the reproductive state in women: K cycles of secretion were irregular in menstruating and lactating women. The time of peak glucose secretion changed and the concentration increased acutely three- to ninefold during menstruation.[19] Significant changes in salivary composition occur with ovulation in women: calcium and sodium levels decrease and potassium increases.[20] Salivary peroxidase activities are highest just before ovulation.[21] Oral contraceptives enhance the buffering capacity of saliva.[22] Menopause does not influence salivary gland function in healthy women, nor does hormonal replacement therapy.[23] It is likely that complaints of burning mouth in elderly women are more related to medication than to the menopausal state.[24]

Saliva is a more and more popular medium in which to assess various aspects of endocrine status and disease states. Salivary progesterone levels are now widely used to assess female ovarian function.[25] One of the most important consequences of salivary monitoring in individual women was to show that there are fluctuations in normal human ovarian function, even when menstruation is regular and still present. Such variations are seasonal, possibly in response to work loads.[26]

References

1. Kleinberg I, Westbay G. Salivary and metabolic factors involved in oral malodor formation. J Periodontal. 1992;63:768-775.
2. Berg M, Burrill DY, Fosdick LS. Chemical studies in periodontal disease. II. Putrefactive organisms in the mouth. J Dent Res. 1946;25:73-81.
3. McNamara TF, Alexander JF, Lee M. The role of microorganisms in the production of oral malodor. Oral Surg Oral Med Oral Pathol 1972;34:41-48.
4. Salako NO, Ryan C, Kleinberg I. Comparison of the acidogenicities of galactose and glucose. J Dent Res. 1988;67:203.
5. Traudt M, Kleinberg I. Bacteria in human dental plaque responsible for its oxygen uptake activity. J Dent Res. 1988;67:204.
6. Converso C, Kleinberg I. Degradation of salivary proteins by pure cultures of oral bacteria. J Dent Res. 1988;67:203. Abstract.
7. Shiota T, Kunekl MF Jr. In vitro chemical and bacterial changes in saliva. J Dent Res. 1958;37:780-787.
8. Stralfors A. An investigation of the respiratory activities of oral bacteria. Acta Odontol Scand. 1956;14:153-186.
9. Dawes C. Physiological factors affecting salivary flow rate, oral sugar clearance and the sensation of dry mouth in man. J Dent Res. 1987;66:648-653.
10. Dawes C. A mathematical model of salivary clearance of sugar from the oral cavity. Caries Res. 1983;17:321-334.
11. Meurman JH, Rantonen P. Salivary flow rate, buffering capacity and yeast counts in 187 consecutive adult patients from Kuopio, Finland. Scand J Dent Res. 1994;102:229-234.
12. Johansson A. Kiliaridis S, Haraldson T, Omar R, Carolsson GE. Covariation of some factors associated with occlusal tooth wear in a selected high-wear sample. Scan J Dent Res. 1993;101:398-406.
13. Friedlander AH, West LJ. Dental management of the patient with major depression. Oral Surg Oral Med

Oral Pathol. 1991;71:573-578.

14. Sreebny LM, Yu A, Green A, Valdini A. Diabetes Care. 1992;15:900-904.

15. Cherry-Peppers G, Sorkin J, Andres R, Baum BJ, Ship JA. Salivary gland function and glucose metabolic status. Gerontol. 1992;47:130-134.

16. Fox PC. Saliva and salivary gland alterations on HIV infection. J Am Dent Assoc. 1991;122:46-48.

17. Fox PC. Salivary monitoring in oral diseases. Annals N Y Acad Sci. 1993;694:234-237.

18. Atwood CS, James IR, Keil U, Roberts NK, Hartmann PE. Circadian changes in salivary constituents and conductivity in women and men. Chronobiologia. 1991;18:125-140.

19. Prosser CG, Hartmann PE. Saliva and breast milk composition during the menstrual cycle of women. Aust J Exp Biol Med Sci. 1983;61:265-275.

20. Puskulian L. Salivary electrolyte changes during the normal menstrual cycle. J Dent Res. 1972;51:1212-1216.

21. Tenovuo J, Laine M, Soderling E, Irjala K. Evaluation of salivary markers during the menstrual cycle: peroxidase, protein and electrolytes. Biochem Med. 1981;25:337-345.

22. Laine M, Pienihakkinen K, Ojanotko Harri A, Tenovuo J. Effects of low dose oral contraceptives on female whole saliva. Arch Oral Biol. 1991;36:549-552.

23. Ship JA, Patton LL, Tylenda CA. An assessment of salivary functioning in healthy premenopausal and postmenopausal females. J Gerontol. 1991;46:M11-15.

24. Parvinen T, Parvinen I, Larmas M. Stimulated salivary flow rate, pH and lactobacillus and yeast concentrations in medicated persons. Scand J Dent Res. 1984;92:524-532.

25. Ellison PT. Salivary steroids and natural variation in human ovarian function. Annals N Y Acad Sci. 1994; 709:287-298.

26. Panter-Brick C. Seasonality and levels of energy expenditure during pregnancy and lactation for rural Nepali women. Am J Clin Nutr. 1993;57:620-628.

Chapter 10

The Urinary and
Reproductive Tracts

The Urinary Tract

The anatomy of the urogenital tract in women and men is significantly different. The female urethra is about an inch and a half long and is wider and more distensible than that of the male. These features of urethral anatomy predispose women to much more frequent urinary tract infections than are seen in men, in whom the urethra is almost five times longer than in women. The female urethra leads from the bladder and opens as a slit-like orifice to the outside world immediately in front of the vaginal orifice. Posteriorly, it is partially embedded in the anterior vaginal wall. Therefore, anything that distends the vagina can potentially stretch and bruise the urethra. The proximity of the urethral opening to the vaginal and anal orifices is another risk factor for frequent urinary tract infection in women. Alteration of protective vaginal flora by antibiotics given for other infections, mechanical trauma during intercourse, or introduction of bacteria from the anal area to the urethral zone by sexual activity or poor toilet habits all predispose women to infection.

A muscular coat, continuous with the bladder musculature, extends almost to the lower third of the urethra, where it is largely replaced by fibrous tissue. There are two sets of glands (the glands of Skene) near the lower end of the urethra. Their ducts coalesce to form the two paraurethral ducts that open into two individual orifices. Most embryologists and anatomists view these glands as homologous with the male prostate. In some women, at the moment of orgasm, fluid is expressed from the paraurethral ducts; again, this fluid is analogous to the male ejaculate.

Urethral stricture is often seen with chronic urethritis; in women, repeated infections produce a diffuse thickening and narrowing of the urethra. In men, on the other hand, stricture is generally a localized circular narrowing or scarring secondary to gonorrheal infection. While strictures in females are very rarely severe enough to cause residual retention of urine, women suffer frequency, pain (which may be referred to the urethra, bladder, sacral, inguinal or the lumbar region), burning, urgency and mild incontinence.

A detailed listing of all the diseases that may attack the urethra and bladder in women is not germane to this discussion. What is useful to review is the most frequent etiologic agents for urinary tract infection and their optimal treatment. A discussion of urinary incontinence is also relevant.

Urinary Tract Infection (UTI) in Women in the United States

The **cost** of urinary tract infection in American women is significant. Females have a 10-20% risk of having a UTI in their lifetime. Treatment for an episode of acute cystitis costs approximately $140; the annual cost in ambulatory patients is $1 billion, and women make 5.2 million office visits each year for this ailment.[1] Hospitalizations, which require an average of 7 days, amount to well over 100,000 a year; an average charge for such a stay is $3,164 ± $1,197.[2a,2b]

The etiologic agents in cystitis vary with the acuteness or chronicity of the process and with the age of the patient. In young women with acute uncomplicated cystitis, *Escherichia coli* (*E. coli*) cause 80%, *Staphylococcus saprophyticus*, 10-15%, and other pathogens (*Klebsiella, Proteus mirabilis*, etc.) the remainder of the infections.[3]

The two most common infective agents originate in the gastrointestinal tract. They migrate anteriorly to cause an ascending infection. The risk factors for infection include sexual intercourse, delayed urination following intercourse, the use of a diaphragm and a history of a previous urinary tract infection.[4] Spermicide use is also a risk factor for acute cystitis. As is the case with some antimicrobials, spermicide modifies vaginal flora, allowing *E. coli* to colonize the urinary tract and facilitate infection.[5] However, in complicated urinary tract infections that occur in women with some abnormality of the urinary tract or in women with antibiotic-resistant pathogens, the spectrum of infecting agents changes. *E. coli* causes about 35% of these infections. Other agents, including *Enterococcus faecalis* (16%), *Proteus* (13%), *Klebsiella* (7%), *Pseudomonas* (5%), *Enterobacter* (2.5%), *Staphyloccocus aureus* (4%) and *Staphylococcus epidermidis* (12%) cause the remainder.[6]

There have been two significant changes in the recommended treatment of urinary tract infection over the past few years: **the course of medication is much shorter** and culture/susceptibility testing is usually unnecessary, particularly in acute and uncomplicated infections. In most cases, the choice of agents does not vary with the identity of the pathogen causing the urinary tract infection (acute uncomplicated versus complicated) but the duration of therapy does, ranging from 3 days in the treatment of acute uncomplicated cystitis to 14 days in mild to moderate acute uncomplicated pyelonephritis and urinary tract infection. Trimethoprim-sulfamethoxazole or the quinolones are the agents of choice because of their broad spectrum and their demonstrated efficacy.

The second important change in treatment is the fact that **parenteral therapy is not necessary in all cases** of pyelonephritis and complicated UTI because of the effectiveness of oral agents. This has resulted in much shorter hospitalizations, because even when parenteral therapy is indicated initially (usually only if nausea and vomiting prevents taking oral agents or the patient is very ill, with high fever and dehydration), the patient can be switched after 48 hours to the oral form of the drug and managed on an out-patient basis.

Urinary Tract Problems in the Postmenopausal Woman

The urethra is lined with multiple layers of squamous epithelial cells, and the mucosa is thrown up into longitudinal folds. With menopause, the vaginal and urethral mucosa become much thinner and the urethra shortens even further, with consequent increased vulnerability to infection and, often, a sensation of urethral burning even when the patient is not urinating. Frank dysuria is also a common complaint, even in the absence of infection. Effective treatment is usually estrogen replacement, either systemic or by local application of estrogen cream.

Urinary incontinence in older women is a significant economic and personal burden. Ten to twenty percent of elderly women living in the community, 20-40% of hospitalized women and over 50% of nursing home females are incontinent.[7,8] Indeed, the reported incidence is probably an underestimate; embarrassment prevents many patients from admitting to incontinence.[9] The annual direct cost of urinary incontinence in this country is estimated to be over $10 billion[10] and the emotional impact is tremendous for the patient and her family. Social isolation is common.[11]

Urinary incontinence in the aging woman is often multifactorial. With age, the contractile ability of the bladder during urination diminishes and residual urine volume increases. This, along with the shortened urethra of estrogen-deprived states, promotes infection. Acute or reversible incontinence is the result of a systemic problem: delirium, medication (such as atropine), restricted mobility or stool impaction are common causes.

Overflow Incontinence

Chronic incontinence may be due to relaxation of the muscles of the pelvic floor and/or malfunction of the detrusor muscle, which provides the force for bladder emptying during urination. Under normal circumstances, sensations of bladder fullness produce a reflex spinal arc which prompts a strong detrusor contraction resulting in urination. In the intact individual, cortical suppression of this spinal arc prevents urination. If inhibitory pathways from the cortex are damaged or destroyed, the detrusor muscle contracts reflexly simply in response to bladder distention. This condition of "detrusor instability" is responsible for almost 70% of incontinence in the elderly. Treatment is aimed at lessening the force of detrusor contraction: imipramine, 25 mg at bedtime, or calcium channel blockers improve continence.

Stress Incontinence

Relaxation of pelvic floor muscles in the post-menopausal woman, particularly in one who has had children, results in urinary losses under conditions of increased intra-abdominal pressure, i.e, coughing and laughing. Relaxation of the pelvic floor allows the bladder to drop from its normal position above the pelvic diaphragm, changing the normal urethrovesical angle and shortening the length of the urethra, both of which are important in maintaining closure of the urethral sphincter.

Sphincteric incompetence is another important cause of stress incontinence; this is treated with systemic or local estrogen replacement. Local collagen injection may also be effective in a selected group of patients. A new electrical stimulation device developed by Dr. Peter K. Sand (at Northwestern University Medical School) produced significant improvement of pelvic muscle strength and reduced the severity of stress incontinence in 40-90% of treated patients. The device is made of silicone rubber with carbon electrodes and is used twice a day for 15 minutes the first 4 weeks, and 30 minutes twice a day for the remainder of the 12-week study.[12]

The Vagina

The normal vaginal mucosa is populated by a group of microorganisms that coexist with the host in a mutually beneficial kind of dynamic equilibrium. There are several fundamental principles that govern the relationship between the vagina and its colonies of microorganisms: (1) The composition and number of flora are a reflection of the characteristics of the host tissue. (2) Any alteration in the condition of the tissue will impact on the type and number of floral species. Estrogenic stimulation of the rat vagina, for example, increased bacterial counts by 10,000-fold within 24 hours or less.[13,14] In fact, the impact of hormonally altered mucosa may not be just quantitative, but actually enable some species to colonize the vagina. Oophorectomized rats who received continuous estrogen stimulation could be colonized by *Candida albicans*,[15] while normally cycling rats were never colonized by yeast.[16]

The normal vaginal flora include several species of bacteria, both gram-positive and gram-negative, as well as anaerobic and facultatively anaerobic species. **The view that the vagina is colonized almost exclusively by lactobacilli is incorrect**.[17] What may be correct, though, is that the lactic acid produced by lactobacilli restricts the growth of other organisms by making vaginal pH acid. Some strains also produce hydrogen peroxide, which may help them successfully colonize the vagina.[18] The symbiotic interaction between flora is also probably important; one species may produce a needed nutrient for another species ("cross feeding") or provide protection from a host protective factor. Anything that alters the normal vaginal flora opens the door to colonization of the mucosa by a harmful invader; these include systemic antibiotics, abortion, intercurrent infection in the area and, some believe, douching.

The vaginal epithelium is constantly being renewed by cells that divide in the basal layer and mature toward the lumen until they become effete and are sloughed off into the vaginal canal, carrying with them any attached microorganisms. The rate at which this occurs is driven by estrogen. The vaginal epithelium in humans undergoes virtually constant stimulation by estrogen during the menstrual cycle; the secretion of progesterone occurs simultaneously with estrogen in the follicular phase. The ability of lactobacillus to colonize the human vagina is closely related to estrogen: in female infants who still have transplacentally acquired estrogen, lactobacillus is abundant; it diminishes until menarche, flourishes again during the reproductive years (most markedly during pregnancy) and diminishes after menopause.[19] The mechanism of the dependence of lactobacillus on estrogen is still incompletely understood, but part of the interaction may depend on the production of glycogen in the estrogen-stimulated vaginal epithelium; the bacillus ferments the glycogen, produces acid and thereby restricts flora to acid-tolerant species. The impact of progesterone on the type and number of vaginal flora is unknown. How the flora extract nutrients from the vaginal epithelium is of considerable interest; it may be from the products of degradation of sloughed epithelial cells. Nutrients may also be contained in serous transudates, menstrual fluid and secretory products from the endocervical and Bartholin's glands in the vagina. In a study of specimens from 44 subjects, Larsen determined that vaginal carbohydrate and protein concentrations were much lower in yeast colonized subjects than in noncolonized women.[20] Micronutrients such as iron and vitamins may also be important; iron may enhance the virulence of various pathogens which obtain the element by producing transferrin-binding proteins which acquire iron for the bacterium by taking it from host transferrin.[21,22] Other work has demonstrated that procedures likely to introduce blood into the vaginal vault markedly increased the numbers of some of the normal flora.[23]

The oxidation-reduction potential of the vagina is low; this may be the reason for the predominance of anaerobic bacteria, which outnumber facultative species by a factor of 10.[24] The normal pH of the vagina is between 4-4.5 and limits the flora to acidophilic or aciduric species like the lactobacillus. The vagina itself creates this low pH; infant girls who are not yet colonized have an acid pH.

Fluctuation of leukocytic infiltration of the vaginal mucosa occurs with the menstrual cycle and has an important impact on the number of bacterial colonies in the vagina.[25]

Some investigators have suggested using active yogurt cultures to produce favorable vaginal colonization. This idea becomes even more attractive when one considers that if lactobacilli are selectively removed from the vagina, yeast overgrowth occurs. The yeast is quickly ejected from tissue if the lactobacillus can recolonize. Reservations about the usefulness of artificial replacement of lactobacillus include the conviction of some that a local immune response may be raised against instilled organisms. They also point out that the new organisms may not be adapted to the vaginal mucosal environment.[26]

Both pathogenic and benign organisms need an attachment mechanism in order to colonize the mucosa. This is accomplished by the pilus of the bacterium. *Nesseria gonorrhoeae* (*N. gonorrhoeae*) pili attach only to the cuboidal epithelium of the cervix; normal flora have surface structures that enable them to bind to epithelial cells. The nature and number of epithelial cell attachment sites in the host may vary, explaining why some women are more vulnerable to yeast infections, for example, than others.

Douching: Users, Preparations and Consequences

Estimates of the numbers of American women who regularly practice vaginal douching vary between 20 million and 67 million.[27] The question of whether or not douching itself produces vaginal and pelvic infection, or is simply the attempt of women to treat existing infections or to combat unsafe sexual practices and, thus, is simply **associated** with reproductive tract infection, is unsettled.[28] Nevertheless, women who douched during the 3 months prior to a recent survey had a relative risk (RR) of 2.1 for pelvic inflammatory disease after controlling for other measured risk factors; those who douched more often had a greater risk (RR 3.9) than those who douched less often (RR 1.8).[29]

The preparation used for douching may have an impact on infection: physiologic saline transiently reduced the total bacterial count of normal vaginal flora; if one used a preparation containing acetic acid, the reduction was still more marked. The greatest impact on total counts was from a povidone-iodine preparation. In some women, the use of this preparation might decrease the numbers of normal flora to the point where colonization by a pathogen is facilitated.[30] Other studies, however, confirm the remarkable stability of normal vaginal flora. Monif and colleagues showed that within 24 hours of using an iodophor douche, the vaginal flora reverted to its normal state.[31] Shubair and colleagues demonstrated that a douche containing chlorhexidine gluconate produced absolutely no change in the nature or number of normal vaginal flora.[32] There may be some advantages to douching with a mildly alkaline solution; Everhardt and colleagues showed that such a preparation lessened the viscoelasticity of cervical mucous and improved the sperm penetration index in infertile couples.[33]

In a survey of 8,450 women in the United States between the ages of 15 to 44, two thirds of the women who douched were black and only a third were white. The practice was least frequent among 15 to 19 year olds and most frequent in 20 to 24 year olds. It was more common among women who lived in poverty and those with less than a high school education (who were four times more like to report douching as those with 16 or more years of schooling). There was a significantly higher incidence of pelvic inflammatory disease among those who douched; women with less than one and those with ten or more partners were less likely to douche than others.[34]

There are conflicting opinions about whether vaginal douching increases the risk for ectopic pregnancy. Some investigators believe that it does not,[35] while others have found a modestly increased incidence (RR 1.3) of ectopic pregnancy in those who douched.[36]

In another study, frequent douching (more than once a week) was associated with a significantly increased RR (4.7) for cervical cancer.[37]

Recurrent Vulvovaginal Candida Infection

There is no good epidemiological profile of the woman who is susceptible to recurrent vaginal candidiasis in whom diabetes, the use of antibiotics, steroids or immuno-suppression are not factors. Spinillo and colleagues studied 86 patients with the problem.[38] They point out that while the use of the high-estrogen contraceptive pill was associated with this problem, the lower dose pill has not been found to cause vulnerability to candidal vaginitis. Commercially available cleansing solutions for the external genitalia or for vaginal douching were both significant risk factors. The likelihood of infection was proportional to the number of sexual encounters. Two hypotheses have been suggested for this "coitus related" candidal vaginitis: an allergic response to the partner's semen,[39] and/or microscopic injury associated with the mechanical trauma of coitus.[40]

Reinfection is usually associated with different strains of candida; Spinillo's paper suggests that previous antimycotic therapy might have selected out different (and also pathogenic) strains of candida.

Pelvic Inflammatory Disease

Pelvic inflammatory disease (PID) cost $4.2 billion in 1990 ($2.7 billion in direct costs and $1.5 billion attributable to lost productivity). Projected costs for the year 2000 are over $9 billion.[41] The personal cost is significant as well; 25% of women with PID will have one or more serious, long-term sequelae, including tubal infertility and ectopic pregnancy.[41] One million new cases are diagnosed annually,[42] and this is probably fewer than actually exist because the profile of symptoms of PID is changing dramatically.[43] In the past two decades, symptoms have changed from acute pelvic pain, fever and elevated white blood cell count, to much milder manifestations in many patients: abnormal bleeding, dyspareunia, or vaginal discharge. Some women have no symptoms at all.[44] This change in the clinical profile is directly attributable to the changing nature of the etiologic agent in PID; once almost exclusively the gonococcus, the emerging importance of chlamydia and other organisms as infectious agents is now a significant factor.

Two thirds of the cases of PID are caused by sexually transmitted organisms, *Neisseria gonorrhoeae* and *Chlamydia trachomatis*.[45] *Chlamydia trachomatis* is now the most frequent cause of bacterial STD in the United States.[46] It is particularly prevalent among the 3 to 6 million adolescents (infecting 9-35%) who develop STD each year. The fact that 30-70% of these adolescents experience no symptoms is of even more concern.[47] Prompt treatment of the infection is essential: intervention within the first 48 hours of infection prevents the infertility that is so often the consequence of the infection.

Bacterial vaginosis is a possible cause of and at least a facilitator in about a third of cases of pelvic inflammatory disease and is the result of infection with a variety of organisms such as prevotela and peptostreptococci.[48]

Effective treatment of PID depends on early intervention. Monotherapy regimens for 10 days, particularly with quinolones, are effective,[49] and recent recommendations from the Centers for Disease Control and Prevention (CDC) make oral therapy an option for the first time. The CDC recommends adding either clindamycin or metronidazole to cover anaerobic organisms.[50] Other regimens (ampicillin/sulbactam, ineffective against *Chlamydia trachomatis* and cefoxitin-probenecid-doxycycline, ineffective against *N. gonorrhoeae*) are not always effective, particularly in the absence of accurate identification of the etiologic agent(s) of infection.[51]

Effective prevention of PID requires a number of interventions. A recent survey of over 10,500 young adults (aged 14-21) showed that 44% of 14-17 year olds and 82% of 18-21 year olds had had sexual intercourse; of these, 13% of the younger group and 41% of the older group had more than four partners within a year. Forty-two percent and 63%, respectively, failed to use condoms.[52] Compliance with treatment programs is another major problem. In a recent study, only 63.4% of outpatients completed a standard 7-day regimen of antibiotics,[53] and a mere 43% returned to clinic for follow-up.[54] Appropriate education, the use of barrier methods of protection, and compliance with medical regimens are all important, as are protective periodic examinations of people at high risk like prostitutes.[54] Sex partners of women with acute PID should be treated empirically for infection because testing is insensitive in asymptomatic men.[55]

References

1. Washington E. A modern perspective: the magnitude of genitourinary infections in 1994. In: Genitourinary

Infections in Women: Update on Urinary Tract Infections and Pelvic Inflammatory Disease. University of Wisconsin Medical School. August, 1994.

2a. Johnson JR, Stamm WE. Urinary tract infections in women: diagnosis and treatment. Ann Intern Med. 1989;111:906-917.

2b. Safrin S, Siegel D, Black D. Pyelonephritis in adult women: inpatient versus outpatient therapy. Am J Med. 1988;85:793-798.

3. Stamm WE, Hooton TM. Management of urinary tract infections in adults. N Eng J Med. 1993;329:1328-1334.

4. Strom BL, Collins M, West SL, Kreisberg J, Weller S. Sexual activity, contraceptive use, and other risk factors for symptomatic and asymptomatic bacteriuria: a case-control study. Ann Intern Med. 1987;107:816-823.

5. Hooton TM, Hillier S, Johnson C, Roberts PL, Stamm WE. *Escherichia coli* bacteriuria and contraceptive method. JAMA. 1991;265:64-69.

6. Naber KG. Use of quinolones in urinary tract infections and prostatitis. Rev Infect Dis. 1989;ll(suppl 5):S1321-S1330.

7. Diokno AC, Brok BM, Brown MB, Herzog AR. Prevalence of urinary incontinence and other urologic symptoms in the noninstitutionalized elderly. J Urol. 1986;1361:1022.

8. Harris T, Guralnik J, Medans J. The national health and nutrition examination survey I, follow-up: prevalence and correlates of urinary incontinence in community-dwelling elders. Presentation at the 39th Annual Scientific Meeting of the Gerontologic Society of America. Chicago: 1986.

9. Herzog AR. Prevalence and incidence in a community dwelling population. Urinary Incontinence NIH Consensus Conference. 1988:14-21.

10. Hu T. Impact of urinary incontinence on health care costs. Urinary Incontinence NIH Consensus Conference. 1988:33-34.

11. Wyman JF, Harkins SW, McClish DK, et al. Psychosocial impact of incontinence in the communi-

ty dwelling population. Urinary Incontinence NIH Consensus Conference. 1988:22-28.

12. Mechcatie E. Women's health: electrical stimulation is nonsurgical alternative for stress incontinence. Reported in Internal Medicine News and Cardiology News. 1994:16.

13. Larsen B, Markoveta AJ, Galask RP. Quantitative alterations of the genital microflora of female rats in relation to the estrous cycle. J Infect Dis. 1976;134:486.

14. Larsen B, Markoveta AJ, Galask RP. Scanning electron microscopy of vaginal colonization. App Environ Microbiol. 1977;33:470.

15. Larsen B, Galask RP. Influence of estrogen and normal flora on vaginal candidiasis in the rat. J Reprod Med. 1984;29:863.

16. Larsen B, Markoveta AJ, Galask RP. The bacterial flora of the female rat genital tract. Proc Soc Exp Biol Med. 1976;151:571-574.

17. Larsen B. Normal genital microflora. In: Keith LG, Berger GS, Edelman DA, eds. Infections and Reproductive Health. Vol. 1. Lancaster, UK: MTP; 1985:3.

18. Eschenback DA, Davick PR, Williams BL, et al. Prevalence of hydrogen peroxide-producing lactobacillus species in normal women and women with bacterial vaginosis. J Clin Microbiol. 1989;27:251.

19. Goplerud CP, Ohn MJ, Galask RP. Aerobic and anaerobic flora of the cervix during pregnancy and puerperium. Am J Obstet Gynecol. 1976;126:858.

20. Larsen B. Vaginal flora in health and disease. Clin Obstet Gynecol. 1993;36:107-121.

21. Gonzalez GC, Caamano DL, Schryvers AB. Identification and characterization of a porcine-specific transferrin receptor in Actinobacillus pleuropneumoniae. Mol Microbiol. 1990;4:1173.

22. Morton DJ, Williams P. Siderophore-independent acquisition of transferrin-bound iron by Haemophilus influenza type B. J Gen Microbiol. 1990;136:927-933.

23. Grossman JH III, Adams RL, Hierholzer WJ Jr.

Epidemiologic surveillance during a clinical trial of antibiotic prophylaxsis in pelvic surgery. Am J Obstet Gynecol. 1977;128:690-692.

24. Bartlett JG, Onderdonk AB, Drude E, et al. Quantitative bacteriology of the vaginal flora. J Infect Dis. 1977;136:271-277.

25. Larsen B, Markcoveta AJ, Galask RP. Role of estrogen in controlling the genital microflora of female rats. Appl Environ Microbiol. 1977;34:534-540.

26. Larsen B. Vaginal flora in health and disease. Clin Obstet Gynecol. 1993;36:107-121.

27. Rosenberg MJ, Phillips RS, Holmes HD. Vaginal douching: who and why? J Reprod Med. 1991;36:753-758.

28. Rosenberg MJ, Phillips RS. Does douching promote ascending infection? J Reprod Med. 1992;37:930-938.

29. Scholes D, Daling JR, Stercachis A, Weiss NS, Wang SP, Gravston JT. Vaginal douching as a risk factor for acute pelvic inflammatory disease. Obstet Gynecol. 1993;81:601-606.

30. Onderdonk AB, Delaney ML, Kinkson PL, DuBois AM. Quantitative and qualitative effects of douche preparations on vaginal microflora. Obstet Gynecol. 1992;80:333-338.

31. Monif GRG, Thompson JL, Stephens JD, et al. Quantitative and qualitative effects of povidone-iodine liquid and gel on the aerobic and anaerobic flora of the female genital tract. Am J Obstet Gynecol. 1980;137:432.

32. Shubair M, Stanek R, White S, Larsen B. Effects of chlorhexidine douche on normal vaginal flora. Gynecol Obstet Invest. 1992;34:229-233.

33. Everhardt E, Dony JM, Janse H, Lemmens WA, Doesburg WH. Improvement of cervical mucous viscoelasticity and sperm penetration with sodium bicarbonate douching. Hum Reprod. 1990;5:133-137.

34. Aral SO, Mosher WD, Cates W Jr. Vaginal douching among women of reproductive age in the United States: 1988. Am J Public Health. 1992;82:210-214.

35. Phillips RS, Tuomala RE, Feldblum PJ, Schacter J,

Rosenberg MJ, Aronson MD. The effect of cigarette smoking, *Chlamydia trachomatis* infection and vaginal douching on ectopic pregnancy. Obstet Gynecol. 1992;79:85-90.

36. Daling JR, Weiss NS, Schwartz SM, Steroachis A, Wang SP, Foy H, Chu J, McKnight B, Grayston JT. Vaginal douching and the risk of tubal pregnancy. Epidemiology. 1991;2:40-48.

37. Gardner JW, Schuman KL, Slattery ML, Sanborn JS, Abbott TM, Overall JC Jr. Is vaginal douching related to cervical carcinoma? Am J Epidemiol. 1991;133:368-375.

38. Spinillo A, Pizzoli G, Colonna L, Nicoa, S, DeSeta F, Guaschino S. Epidemiologic characteristics of women with idiopathic recurrent vulvovaginal candidiasis. Obstet Gynecol. 1993;81:721-727.

39. Witkin SS. Immunologic factors influencing suscepti-bility to recurrent candidal vaginitis. Clin Obset Gynecol. 1991;34:662-668.

40. Lossick JG. Sexually transmitted vaginitis. Urol Clin North Am. 1984;11:141-153.

41. Washington AE, Katz P. Cost of and payment source for pelvic inflammatory disease: trends and projections 1983 through 2000. JAMA. 1991;266:2565-2569.

42. Rolfs RT, Balaid EI, Zaidi AA. Pelvic inflammatory dis-ease: trends in hospitalizations and office visits, 1979 through 1988. Am J Obstet Gynecol. 1992;166:983-990.

43. Kahn JG, Walker CK, Washington AE, Landers DV, Sweet RL. Diagnosing pelvic inflammatory disease: a comprehensive analysis and consideration for devel-oping a new model. JAMA. 1991;266:2594-2611.

44. Centers for Disease Control and Prevention. 1993: Sexually transmitted diseases treatment guidelines. Morb Mortal Wkly Rep. 1993;42(RR-14):1-102.

45. Sweet RL. Changing etiology of PID. In: Genitourinary Infections in Women: Update on Urinary Tract Infections and Pelvic Inflammatory Disease. Consensus Conference Proceedings. Health Learning Systems, Inc. 1994:11.

46. Toomey KE, Barnes RC. Treatment of *Chlamydia tra-*

chomatis genital infection. Rev Infect Dis. 1990;12(suppl 6):S645-S655.

47. Adger H, DeAngelis CD. Adolescent medicine. JAMA. 1994;271:1851-1853.

48. Paavonen J, Teisala K, Heinonen PK, et al. Microbiological and histopathological findings in acute pelvic inflammatory disease. Br J Obstet Gynaecol. 1987;94:454-460.

49. Soper DE, Brockwell NJ, Dalton HP. Microbial etiology of urban emergency department acute salpingitis: treatment with ofloxacin. Am J Obstet Gynecol. 1992;167:653-660.

50. Walker CK. PID decision analysis, assessment parameters and outcomes. In: Genitourinary Infections in Women: Update on Urinary Tract Infections and Pelvic Inflammatory Disease. Consensus Conference Proceedings. Health Learning Systems, Inc. 1994:21.

51. Kosseim M, Ronald A, Plummer FA, D'Costa L, Brunham RC. Treatment of acute pelvic inflammatory disease in the ambulatory setting: trial of cefoxitin and doxycycline versus ampicillin-sulbactam. Antimicrob Agents Chemother. 1991;35:1651-1656.

52. Kann L, Warren CW, Harris WA, et al. Youth risk behavior surveillance: United States 1993. Morb Mortal Wkly Rep. CDC Surveill Summ. 1995;44(1):1-56.

53. Katz BP, Zwickl BW, Caine VA, Jones RB. Complaince with antibiotic therapy for *Chlamydia trachomatis* and *Neisseria Gonorrhoeae*. Sex Transm Dis. 1992;19:351-354.

54. Solomon MZ, DeJong W. The impact of a clinic-based educational videotape on knowledge and treatment behavior of men with gonorrhea. Sex Transm Dis. 1988;15:127-132.

55. Plummer FA, Ngugi EN. Prostitutes and their clients in the epidemiology and control of sexually transmitted diseases. In: Holmes KK, Mardh P-A, Sparling PF, Wiesner PJ, eds. Sexually Transmitted Diseases. 2nd ed. New York: McGraw-Hill Information Services Co; 1990:71-76.

Index